The
HIDDEN PLACES

of
GLOUCESTERSHIRE

including the Forest of Dean and the Cotswolds

Edited by
Shane Scott

Published by:
Travel Publishing Ltd
7a Apollo House, Calleva Park
Aldermaston, Berks, RG7 8TN

ISBN 1-902-00700-X
© Travel Publishing Ltd 1997

OTHER TITLES IN THE HIDDEN PLACES SERIES

Typesetting by: J Billing, Great Sutton, South Wirral
Printing by: Nuffield Press, Abingdon
Cartography by: Oxford Cartographers, Eynsham, Oxford

Line Drawings: Sarah Bird

Editor: Shane Scott

Cover :   Clare Hackney

   Born in 1961, Clare was educated at West Surrey College of Art and Design as well as
   studying at Kingston University. She runs her own private water-colour school based in
   Surrey and has exhibited both in the UK and internationally. The cover is taken from an
   original water-colour of Chipping Campden, Gloucestershire.

Foreword

THE HIDDEN PLACES is designed to be an easy to use guide, taking you, in this instance, on a gentle tour through the beautiful countryside of Gloucestershire. However, our books cover many areas and now encompass most of the British Isles. We have combined interesting descriptions of the well-known and enduring tourist attractions with those more secluded and as yet little known venues, easy to miss unless you know exactly where you are going.

We include hotels, inns, restaurants, tea shops, various types of accommodation, historic houses, museums, gardens, craft centres and general attractions throughout the county of Gloucestershire, together with our research on local history. Most places have a line drawing and a brief description of the services offered. Maps for each chapter can be found at the back of the book. To ensure complete coverage chapter 6 includes the part of Oxfordshire which is generally accepted to be within the Cotswolds area.

We do not include firm prices or award merits. We merely wish to point you to *The Hidden Places* which will hopefully improve your enjoyment of a holiday or business trip and tempt you to return. The places featured in this book will, we are sure, be pleased if you mention that it was *The Hidden Places* that prompted you to visit.

THE HIDDEN PLACES OF
GLOUCESTERSHIRE

CONTENTS

CHAPTER ONE
Royal Forest of Dean

Westbury Court

Puzzle Wood, Coleford

1
Royal Forest of Dean

Introduction

The Royal Forest of Dean is a place with a long and fascinating history. Its geographical location in an area bordered by the Severn estuary to the south and the Wye valley to the west has effectively isolated it from the rest of England and Wales and as a result, it has developed its own unique character which endures to this day. In its time, this ancient forest has been a wild wood, a royal hunting ground, a naval timber reserve, and an important mining and industrial area, and today it provides the visitor with rich and varied landscape with an enchanting timeless atmosphere.

Following the last Ice Age, an area of some 120,000 acres between the rivers Severn, Wye and Leadon became covered with dense deciduous forest which remained relatively undisturbed until around 4000 BC, when the farmers of the New Stone Age began a process of field clearance using their highly-prized flint axes. Gradually, large numbers of trees were felled and the timber used for a variety of purposes, including building materials and fuel. It was also around this time that the process of coppicing was devised, where the new shoots growing from the bases of the felled trees were cultivated to provide a future source of timber.

The Forest of Dean has long been home to a wide variety of animals and birds. Indeed, the presence of deer led to it being designated a royal hunting forest by King Edmund Ironside early in the 11th century. Later that century, King Canute established the Court of Verderers, a body which was given overall responsibility for everything that grew or lived in the forest. This ancient council still meets ten times a year at the Speech

House near Cannop Ponds in a unique building, now part of a hotel, which was built as a courtroom to settle disputes between the foresters and the new wave of iron-founders who began operating in the 17th century.

Iron ore deposits were first discovered in the forest over 2500 years ago along an irregular arc which runs between Staunton and Lydney in the west and south, and Ruspidge and Wigpool in the east and north. These deposits were widely exploited by the ancient Romans, although it wasn't until the Crown allowed areas of the forest to be leased to commercially-motivated entrepreneurs in the 1600s that mineral extraction began to take place on a grand scale.

Far more devastating to the environment, though, was the demand for forest timber to fuel the iron-smelting process. (The timber had first to be converted to charcoal in order to generate the high temperatures required - a need which spawned its own local industry.) At one time as many as 72 furnaces were operating in and around the Forest of Dean, each of which required around 5000 cubic feet of timber to produce a single bar of iron. Such was the scale of resulting deforestation that by the 1660s, the once-magnificent forest had been reduced to a few hundred trees.

Prompted by a serious concern about the shortage of mature oaks for naval shipbuilding, the government finally acted in 1668 by cancelling all leases for mineral extraction and passing the Dean Forest (Reforestation) Act, one of the earliest examples of conservation legislation. This led to an extensive replanting programme which eventually restored the forest to something approaching its original state. The Napoleonic Wars prompted further restocking and by 1840, nearly 20,000 acres had been replanted, mostly with young oaks. However, by the time these trees had reached maturity, steel had replaced timber as the principal shipbuilding material and they were not required. Some examples of the early 19th century replanting can still be seen in the **Cannop Valley Nature Reserve**.

During the Victorian era, another of the Forest of Dean's natural resources, coal, began to be extracted in large quantities. At one time, up to a million tons were removed each year, mostly from open cast workings, and coke was introduced to replace charcoal in the smelting process. However within a few decades, the local smelting industry had again been driven to the brink of extinction by a series of technological advances and competition from other UK iron-producing areas. Large scale coal extraction came to an end in the 1930s, although a few seams are still being worked to this day by groups of 'free miners', individuals who continue to exercise their traditional right to extract minerals from the forest. Although centuries of outcrop mining have left their mark, the forest has gradually reclaimed these surface workings, or *scowles*, often concealing them in a dense covering of moss, trees and lime-loving plants.

Today, the wooded area of the Royal Forest of Dean covers some 27,000 acres and although still under the ownership of the Crown, it has been vested in the Forestry Commission since 1924. Now one of its most successfully managed areas, the Commission has established a large number of waymarked woodland walks, most of which are fully described in an excellent series of leaflets and guides; it has also been responsible for laying out a number of tastefully landscaped picnic areas and car parks. Its principal task, however, has been to manage the commercial woodlands, half of which are planted with broad leaved deciduous trees, predominantly oak with beech, ash and sweet chestnut, with the balance being non-native conifers such as larch, fir and spruce.

Further information on the background and history of the Royal Forest of Dean and its inhabitants can be obtained at the **Dean Heritage Centre** at Lower Soudley, a fascinating living museum which is described more fully on page 28.

LONGHOPE

Our suggested tour of southwest Gloucestershire and the Royal Forest of Dean commences in the village of Longhope, an attractive settlement lying to the south of the A40 Gloucester to Ross-on-Wye road which has interesting open farm specialising in Angora goats. **Blakemore Goat Farm** is open on Wednesdays to Sundays, 10.30am to 5pm, all year round; admission free.

Longhope is also the location of the **Harts Barn Flower and Craft Centre**, an impressive concern which is situated on the A4136 between Longhope and Mitcheldean, only fifteen minutes' drive from Ross-on-Wye. This restored Norman hunting lodge is one of the oldest properties in the Forest, built by William, Duke of Normandy as a place to keep his hounds when he came to hunt the hart. Over the centuries the original hunting lodge has seen a variety of uses as successive generations of Sargeaunts improved, developed and conserved.

When Howard and Linda Duberley took over Harts Barn in 1995, the elegant brick house, with its lovely William and Mary frontage and collection of outbuildings and barns, had served as a dairy farm for 200 years. Now, with the help of sons Edward and Stuart, they have developed it as a regional centre of excellence for high quality arts and crafts. By the time the centre was officially opened by Sir John Harvey Jones in July 1996, much had been achieved. The barns had been tastefully converted into galleries and workshops, and new extensions had been added.

The former coach house is now a dried flower barn where Linda, one of the region's top flower designers, creates beautiful displays of homegrown blooms. She can even organise a complete wedding day here. The sheltered courtyard is surrounded by individual craft workshops showing an amazing range of handmade items, including hand-painted silk scarves and blouses, teddy bears, African sculpture, leather work, horse tack and equestrian needs, original photography, picture-framing, and much more. The old cow house and stable is now an extremely attractive and welcoming tearoom which specialises in delicious hot lunches and cream teas. Harts Barn Flower and Craft Centre is open daily, 10am to 5pm throughout the year (except Christmas and New Year's day), with hours varying according to season.

Harts Barn Flower and Craft Centre, Monmouth Road, Longhope
Tel: 01452 830954 Fax: 01452 831221

MITCHELDEAN

Excellent self-catering accommodation on the northern fringe of the Forest of Dean can be found a couple of miles west of Longhope near the peaceful community of Mitcheldean. **The Granary** is a self-contained detached cottage standing adjacent to Green Farm which lies in quiet woodland overlooking attractive farmland. Thought to be over 250 years old, the cottage is a former dairy and grain store which has been tastefully converted to provide excellent self-catering accommodation with all the modern facilities.

The Granary, Green Farm, Jubilee Road, Mitcheldean
Tel: 01594 544622

Sleeping up to three, there is an attractive lounge with French windows opening out onto the garden, a fully-equipped kitchen, and a large bedroom on the first floor with comfortable Victorian framed beds. Annie Frost from Green Farm is on hand to offer assistance and advice if required, making this the perfect place for a relaxing break in tranquil surroundings.

RUARDEAN

The lovely old village of Ruardean is situated two miles to the northwest of the hamlet of Nailbridge on A4136 Gloucester-Monmouth road. The village church is known for its stone plaque on which two highly-unusual fish are carved. These are thought to have been sculpted by craftsmen from the Herefordshire School of Norman Architecture during the Romanesque period around 1150. The carving is thought to belong to a frieze which was set into one of the church's exterior walls before it was removed in the 13th century, most probably by local people looking for a ready source of building materials. The frieze was considered lost, until seven centuries later, an inspection of a bread oven in a nearby cottage revealed the two fish set into its lining. These have now been returned to the church and can be seen on one of the inside walls near the font.

Carvings, Ruardean Church

UPPER AND LOWER LYDBROOK

From Ruardean, the minor country roads lead westwards towards the two sister villages of Upper and Lower Lydbrook. Although it is hard to imagine today, at one time these two tranquil communities rivalled Sheffield as a producer of pig iron. When the extraction of iron ore and coal was at its height, their position on the northwest fringe of the forest made them ideally suited for the processing of turning ore into metal. Indeed, the first commercially-viable blast furnace in the area was sited here at the beginning of the 17th century.

Lower Lydbrook stands at the point where the River Wye comes closest to the mineral extracting areas of the Forest of Dean and for several centuries, flat-bottomed barges were loaded here with coal bound for Hereford, 25 miles upstream. (Until the completion of a towpath suitable for horses in 1811, the task of hauling the barges against the current was carried out by manpower alone.) This river trade continued until the 1840s, when it was superseded, first by the Gloucester-Hereford Canal, and then the Severn and Wye Railway. Today, the two villages are relatively quiet and secluded and reveal little of their busy industrial past. The house where tragedian actress Sarah Siddons lived as a child can be seen here, along with a number of charming 18th century Georgian buildings.

SYMONDS YAT

A couple of miles due west as the crow flies, though further by road, Symonds Yat is a spectacular outcrop of rock which forms part of Huntsham Hill, the promontory which forces the River Wye to make a striking horseshoe deviation to the north. A popular place which offers magnificent views of the Wye Valley, it is also possible to catch a glimpse of the rare peregrine falcons which inhabit the barren slopes of Yat Rock. This dramatic 500 foot rock is reached along a quarter mile forest trail which can be joined at the Symonds Yat car park. (Refreshments and toilet facilities available during the summer months.)

SYMONDS YAT WEST

On the riverbank below Yat Rock there is an unusual man-powered rope ferry which takes passengers across to Symonds Yat West, a place with some first-rate visitor attractions, including the **Jubilee Park Museum of Mazes**. Run by the Heyes brothers, two keen maze-building enthusiasts, the museum is filled with interesting background information on the art of maze design. It also has an internationally-renowned centrepiece, the Jubilee Puzzle hedge maze, which visitors are encouraged to tackle. The museum is open daily throughout the year, except during January.

Symonds Yat West has a useful visitor centre, and there is also a heritage centre on the nearby Doward hillside. This dramatic stretch of the River Wye is renowned for its leisure and watersports activities, including canoeing, rock climbing, abseiling and even hot-air ballooning, and the surrounding countryside offers some wonderful woodland walks.

At **Goodrich**, one mile to the northeast, the **Wye Valley Farm Park** is a friendly open farm with a good collection of rare and old-fashioned farm animals. A variety of baby animals are born throughout the year which children are encouraged to meet and get to know. (Open daily between Easter and end-October.) Goodrich also has an impressive castle.

An establishment with a great deal to offers its patrons, the **Old Court Hotel** is situated just a few hundred yards from the main A40 within easy walking distance of the peaceful River Wye. Dating from around 1570, previous owners of this superb Tudor manor house include Thomas Gwillim, who fought with General Wolfe at the Battle of Quebec, and John Graves Simcoe, the founder of Toronto. Going through the great oak door into the reception area, it is clear that the character of the building has been carefully preserved. The interior retains a timeless atmosphere of peace and tranquillity, and the twenty guest bedrooms are well appointed and mostly equipped with en-suite facilities.

Old Court Hotel, Symonds Yat West, Near Ross-on-Wye
Tel: 01600 890367 Fax: 01600 890964

The Old Court's Tudor Restaurant offers an intimate setting in which to enjoy excellent cuisine prepared under the watchful eye of the hotel's cordon bleu chef. Or if something lighter is preferred, the Cotswold Bar, with its warming log fires in winter, serves a wide range of hot and cold bar food, along with a full selection of real ales, lagers, wines and spirits. The extensive garden contains a heated swimming pool, and the patio and lawns are the perfect place to sit and relax. This is an ideal base from which to explore the Wye Valley and beyond.

STAUNTON

The village of Staunton can be reached by returning to the A4136 on the eastern side of the river, and then turning west towards Monmouth. This attractive community has a Norman church and a row of charming almshouses which were built in the 1600s with funds donated by Benedict Hall. The church has twice been altered, firstly during the Early English period and again in the 15th century, changes which have left the east window oddly offset from the nave. Look out also for the two stone fonts, one of which is thought to be a converted Roman altar, and the unusual corkscrew staircase which leads up past the pulpit to the belfry door.

Two enormous mystical stones, the **Buck Stone** and the **Suck Stone**, lie a short walk from the centre of Staunton. The famous twelve foot high sandstone monolith known as the Buck Stone can be reached by following a path leading up onto Staunton Meend Common from the White Horse Inn. From here, the views in all directions are breathtaking. The Suck Stone lies along a track from the village across Highmeadow Woods. Look out also for the Bronze Age standing stone which can be seen beside the A4136 at Marion's Cross, just to the east of the village.

Graygill, Staunton, Near Coleford Tel: 01600 712536

Graygill Bed and Breakfast offers a wonderful opportunity for riding enthusiasts with their own pony or horse, since there are stabling facilities and visiting horses are welcome. The home of Mr and Mrs Bond, Graygill is a spacious detached house which is peacefully situated near Staunton on a secluded farm with a large garden, woods and eleven acres of pasture. The house has an extremely comfortable lounge and two en suite bedrooms with a child's cot available. (No smoking in the bedrooms please.) Guests rise to the inviting aroma of breakfast cooking in the kitchen, and can eat as much or as little as they like. With horses and well-controlled pets welcome, this is an ideal location for riding, walking or mountain biking in the beautiful Forest of Dean.

COLEFORD

This lively and aptly-named former mining centre lies two-and-a-half miles southeast of Staunton on the western edge of the Forest of Dean. The town received its royal charter from Charles I in the 17th century in recognition of its loyalty to the crown. By then, it had already grown to be an important iron processing centre, partly because of the availability of local ore deposits, and partly because of the easily obtainable forest timber which was converted to charcoal for use in the smelting process.

Coleford has a special place in metallurgical history for it was here that the Mushets, a father and son team of local free miners, made several discoveries which were to revolutionise the iron and steel industry. Indeed, it was in Coleford that the son, Robert Forester Mushet, discovered how spiegeleisen, an alloy of iron, manganese, silicon and carbon, could be used in the reprocessing of 'burnt iron'. This led him to develop a system for turning molten pig iron directly into steel, a process which predated the more familiar one developed by Sir Henry Bessemer. Tragically however, Robert Mushet allowed his patents to lapse, an oversight which must have resulted in untold financial consequences.

Still regarded as the capital of the Royal Forest of Dean, present day Coleford is a busy commercial centre with an interesting church and a number of notable industrial relics. It is also the home of the **Great Western Railway Museum**, an old GWR goods station dating from 1883 which contains a number of large-scale model steam locomotives and an unusual display of railway photographs and memorabilia. (Open Tuesdays to Sundays and Bank Holiday Mondays, 2.30pm to 5.30pm between Easter and end October; also Saturdays only during the winter months.)

Lying one mile south of Coleford along the B4228 Chepstow road, Lower Perrygrove Farm is the site of ancient woodland mine workings which were imaginatively landscaped during the 19th century. Now known as **Puzzle Wood**, this historic place was a centre for open-cast iron ore mining as long ago as the early Iron Age over 2700 years ago. The site formed part of the famous Lambsquay mine workings during the Roman era, and in 1848, workmen discovered a small cave containing three spherical earthenware jars filled with over 3000 Roman coins dating from the 3rd century AD.

The extraction of iron ore was originally carried out using hand tools only, mostly from high quality deposits lying near the surface. As these were exhausted, miners were forced to look for new seams which often lay trapped beneath layers of solid rock. Before the invention of explosives, the tightly-compressed ore was loosened using the method known as 'fire-setting' which involved lighting fires against the exposed rock face and then dowsing the hot stone with water, causing it to crack.

By the late 19th century when virtually all the ore had been extracted, the fourteen acre Puzzle Wood site was sold to the Turner family who decided to build a network of trails between the steep moss-covered outcrops and mine workings. However, instead of laying out the paths according to a logical plan, they constructed a series of confusing mazes, a fact which accounts for the estate's unusual present day name. In 1981, both Puzzle Wood and Perrygrove Farm were acquired by their present owner, Ray Prosser, who installed an attractive tea garden and souvenir shop. (Open Tuesdays to Sundays and Bank Holiday Mondays, 11am to 6pm between Easter and end October.)

NEWLAND

Before continuing south to Clearwell, it's worth making a short diversion west to visit the charming village of Newland, home of the 'Cathedral of the Forest'. This is the nickname given to the **Church of All Saints**, a massive structure with an aisle almost as wide as its nave and a huge pinnacled tower which needs the support of flying buttresses. Like many other churches in Gloucestershire, it was built during the 13th and 14th centuries and later remodelled by the Victorians. Inside, it has a number of noteworthy features, including a 17th century effigy of a reclining archer and an unusual monumental brass featuring a medieval miner with a candle in his mouth who is holding a pick and a hod.

This is thought to depict Sir John Greyndour, a former Sheriff of Gloucester who, along with a company of miners from the Forest of Dean, accompanied Henry V's forces to France where they helped capture the town of Harfleur. The sturdy artisans of the Forest were often called on by the monarch of the day to operate as an early form of special task force. Indeed, the 'Free Miners of Dean' were given their title by King Edward I after he had successfully put their demolition skills to use undermining the Scottish fortifications around Berwick-on-Tweed.

Newland contains an unusual number of large and well maintained buildings reflecting a stable and prosperous past which seems to have endured into the present. Among the most distinctive of these are the almshouses near the church which were built for eight men and eight women in 1615 and then thoughtfully updated during the 1950s. There is also a charming 16th century pub, the Ostrich, and a Queen Anne farmhouse offering bed and breakfast, Tan House Farm.

CLEARWELL

A two mile journey through the lanes to the southeast of Newland leads to Clearwell, a village containing a number of interesting features, including a 14th century sandstone standing cross, a lovely old inn which is believed to date from the same century, and the extravagantly decorated 19th century **Church of St Peter**. The church was built by Caroline Wyndham, Countess of Dunraven, to replace an earlier building which stood at the other end of the village. She was the last member of her family to live at **Clearwell Castle**, an ornate neo-Gothic mansion which was built in the 1720s by her ancestor, Thomas Wyndham. The house was constructed around an Elizabethan great hall and was used as a base by the notorious Judge Jeffries when he travelled around Wessex trying, and usually sentencing to death or transportation, the supporters of the Duke of Monmouth's ill-fated Pitchfork Rebellion of 1685.

The building was practically destroyed by fire in 1929, and despite being rebuilt, by the 1950s it was again in desperate need of major structural repairs. An unlikely rescuer came in the form of the son of one of the castle gardeners, Frank Yeates, who had been brought up in Clearwell and gone on to earn his fortune as a baker in the North. Yeates bought the neglected estate and proceeded to spend the last years of his life restoring it to its former glory in a labour of love. The castle and grounds now operate as a hotel, although they are open to the public on Sundays only between Easter and October.

The famous **Clearwell Caves** are situated in the heart of the Forest of Dean, a few hundred yards past the pretty chapel on the eastern edge of Clearwell village. These remarkable caves are the site of ancient iron mines which have been worked for over 2500 years from the dawn of the

Iron Age until the present day. The mines were originally a natural cave system which over a long period became filled with rich deposits of iron ore. These deposits have been gradually removed to form a labyrinth of interconnecting passages and chambers, parts of which are still worked.

A substantial part of the workings have now been opened to the public to provide a fascinating all-weather attraction. Nine large caverns, or *churns*, are open to visitors, most of which contain special displays showing the primitive techniques that were employed, and the atrocious working conditions that had to be endured, by mine-workers throughout the ages. For example, it was common practice for children to carry ore up to the surface on their backs in loads weighing up to half-a-hundredweight at a time.

Clearwell Caves, Clearwell, Near Coleford
Tel: 01594 832535

The deepest point in Clearwell Caves normally visited by the public is 100 feet below the surface, although the mine workings descend another

500 feet down into the water table. Visits to some of the deeper levels are possible by special arrangement. The caves are particularly suited to educational visits, and cave formation, local geology and mining history can be studied in detail. The mine workshop contains a collection of heavy engineering machinery used to maintain mining equipment and undertake heritage restoration projects. It also houses a 20 horsepower horizontal engine built by Crossley in 1925, driving a 1925 Ingersol Rand compressor; these can occasionally be seen in operation.

The site also contains an attractive tearoom which is well worth visiting even if just passing for its tempting home-made cakes and interesting collection of mining artefacts. The mine shop stocks mineral samples from all over the world, as well as gifts, books, caving and mining equipment, haematite jewellery and of course, products from the mine. These days the mine is worked to produce educational mineral samples and ochres which are used as pigments in artists' materials and paints. Ochres from the mines can be purchased complete with instructions on how to make earth pigment paints for the home.

ST BRIAVELS

Two miles south of Clearwell Caves, and just to the west of the B4228, lies the impressive village of St Briavels. The community was named after a 5th century Welsh bishop whose name appears in various forms throughout Celtic Wales, Cornwall and Brittany, but at no other place in England. In the Middle Ages, this was an important administrative centre for the Forest of Dean; it was also a major armaments manufacturing centre supplying weapons and ammunition to the Crown. (In 1223, Henry III is believed to have ordered 6000 crossbow bolts (or *quarrels*) from workshops in St Briavels.)

The somewhat oversized village **Church** was built in Norman times to replace a Celtic chapel on the same site. It was significantly enlarged in the 12th and 13th centuries, and further remodelled by the Victorians. Each year on Whit Sunday, the Pound Wall outside the church is the site of a curious custom - the St Briavels Bread and Cheese Ceremony. Following the evensong service, a local forester stands on the wall and throws small pieces of bread and cheese to the assembled villagers below accompanied by the chant, 'St Briavels' water and Whyrl's wheat are the best bread and water King John can ever eat.'

This unique ceremony is thought to have originated over 700 years ago when the inhabitants of St Briavels successfully defended their rights of estover (the right to collect wood from common land) in nearby Hudnalls Wood. As a gesture of gratitude, each villager agreed to pay one penny to the churchwarden towards the feeding of the poor, an act which led to the founding of the bread and cheese ceremony. At one time the event took place inside the church; however, by the middle of the 19th century, the festivities had become so rowdy that it was banished to the wall outside. Local legend has it that the small pieces of bread and cheese bring good luck; they were traditionally cherished by Dean Forest miners who believed they would keep them from harm, much like the bread of holy communion which was said never to perish.

St Briavels also possesses an impressive castle which, perhaps due to its unassailable position on a 900 foot promontory, never saw military action. It was founded in the early 1100s by Henry I and was considerably enlarged during King John's reign in the 13th century when it was used as a hunting lodge. Much of the original structure, including the keep, collapsed during the 18th century; however, the two fortress-like gatehouse towers survive, along with a number of 13th century castle buildings, most of which have been converted to a youth hostel. Parts of the castle are open to the public, including the court and jury rooms, and the castle dungeon whose walls are scored with poignant graffiti. The structure is bordered by a grassy flower-filled moat, creating an atmosphere more suggestive of a fortified country house than a military stronghold.

Blue Barn Bed and Breakfast, St Briavels, Near Coleford
Tel: 01594 530252 or 0589 393192

Those who truly appreciate top quality bed and breakfast accommodation, absolute peace and spectacular views of Tintern Forest and ancient Hudnalls Wood should make a point of finding the **Blue Barn** at St Briavels. Built to a continental design, this lovely home is set in its own grounds on the eastern bank of the picturesque River Wye, midway between Chepstow and Coleford. The bedrooms are beautifully equipped with full en-suite facilities, including both bath and shower.

Carol Parker offers a relaxing private away-from-it-all stay. Her house has a spacious patio, parking area and all-weather tennis court, and the nearby 17 acres of private woodland afford easy access to the Offa's Dyke Path, Wye Valley Walk and a network of footpaths through the beautiful surrounding countryside. The setting offers plenty of scope for walking and exploring, and when guests return after an energetic day, an evening meal is available by arrangement, served on the terrace or inside overlooking the valley. A lovely place to stay, the Blue Barn offers totally peaceful and secluded accommodation, yet it lies only nine miles from the M4 and A40. Unsuitable for smokers.

A narrow lane to the northwest of St Briavels eventually leads down to **Bigsweir Bridge** across the River Wye. This 160 foot single-span structure carries the main A466 Chepstow to Monmouth road and is thought to have been designed either by Thomas Telford or Charles Hollis, the engineer of Windsor Bridge. An unusual toll house stands at its eastern end, while near the other end, **Bigsweir House** can be seen at the foot of Hudnalls Wood.

LLANDOGO

The River Wye forms the border between England and Wales along most of its fifteen mile length between Monmouth and the sea. It's well worth crossing into Gwent and following the A466 south to visit Llandogo, an idyllic little village situated to the west of the main road in a landscape latticed with former horse and donkey tracks which once were the only means of access to the pretty cottages dotted across the hillside.

TINTERN

A couple of miles further south, the dramatic remains of **Tintern Abbey** are situated in an open water meadow beside the River Wye. Though now sadly roofless and beyond repair, this is one of the finest examples of late medieval monastic architecture. Originally founded in 1131 by Cistercian monks from Citeau in France, the remaining buildings date mostly from the 13th to 15th centuries. The walls are still largely intact and feature some fine Gothic detail, including a delicate traceried rose window at the eastern end of the great church which measures over sixty feet in diameter. The abbey site also contains the remains of several smaller buildings, including the chapter house, refectory and kitchens. (Open daily, 9.30am (2pm Sundays) to 6.30pm (4pm in winter), all year round.)

The Cistercians were known for their austere and diligent lifestyle, and intensively farmed the monastic estate using lay brothers to carry out some of the more arduous tasks. Some light relief, however, may have been provided by a predecessor of the present-day Anchor Inn which stood on the nearby riverbank. The route from the inn to the water's edge passes under a 13th century archway which is thought to be the abbey's water gate. On the other side of the river, a natural rock platform known locally as the Devil's Pulpit is where, according to legend, Satan stood to scream insults at the Cistercian monks. Having survived this verbal barrage, Tintern instead fell prey to Henry VIII's Dissolution of the Monasteries, and despite being concealed amongst the steep tree-covered slopes of the Wye Valley, it was abandoned in the mid-16th century.

Tintern Abbey

The **Old Station** at Tintern now functions as a delightful visitor centre. Built during the Victorian era as a halt on the picturesque Wye Valley line, it is surrounded by an attractive picnic area and houses a small exhibition on the history of the local railways. The useful Wye Valley Walk map pack is also available here at a special discounted price. (Open between April and end-October.)

BROCKWEIR

It is possible to cross back into Gloucestershire near the village of Brockweir, a pleasant settlement of white-painted buildings which, prior to the present bridge being completed in 1904, could only be reached from the west bank by ferry. Some of the houses in the village date back to Tudor times and there is also an unusual Moravian chapel which incorporates an assortment of architectural styles from Gothic to Art Nouveau.

Brockweir was once an important river port and boat-building centre. For centuries, small vessels of up to 100 tons were constructed along the riverbank, then in 1824 an improved facility was built which could handle craft of up to 500 tons. Like Lower Lydbrook, this was a place where river barges bound for Monmouth, Hereford and even Hay, were filled with coal and iron ore from the Forest of Dean. These were then hauled upstream by gangs of men harnessed together in teams of eight. Working in relays, it took four such teams to cover the gruelling eight mile stretch of river between Brockweir and Monmouth. It must have been thirsty work for at one time, as many as sixteen pubs were open in the village to serve the combined workforce from the wharves and boatyards. Both boat-building and the river-barge trade were brought to an end by the arrival of the railways in the middle of the 19th century.

The River Wye continues to be well-stocked with salmon thanks to the efforts of a lone Brockweir conservationist, Frank Buckland. Prior to his campaign in the 1920s, salmon netting was allowed along the river's entire length, causing an alarming decline in numbers. However, due to Buckland's efforts, the netting of salmon was strictly controlled below the village and banned altogether above it.

The course of the famous **Offa's Dyke** passes through Brockweir. This great earthwork ditch and rampart was built by Offa, King of Mercia, between AD 757 and 795 to define the western boundary of his kingdom. The original construction ran for nearly 170 miles from the River Severn in the south to the River Dee in the north, the only gaps occurring in areas of dense forest. The dyke was used throughout the medieval period to defend Mercia from Welsh marauders, and during this period, a line of motte and bailey castles was built to strengthen the border defences. Many can still be seen today and those in a suitable state of preservation are generally open to visitors.

Offa's Dyke long distance footpath follows the course of King Offa's 8th century ramparts on the eastern side of the River Wye. The stretch between Monmouth and the sea contains a number of spectacular vantage points which look out across the Wye Valley to the Welsh mountains in the west and the Severn estuary in the south. In particular, there are two outstanding viewpoints, both of which lie within easy reach of the B4228 St Briavels to Chepstow road. The first is from the northern edge of the **Ban-y-gor Rocks**, where the road runs along a ridge above the Wye. There are two dramatic vistas from here: straight down the almost vertical rock face to the river, or eastwards across the Severn towards the Vale of Berkeley and the Cotswolds. The second vantage point can be found three-quarters of a mile further south at **Wintour's Leap**, a massive rocky outcrop which towers 200 feet above the Wye.

At this point, the river is forced to make a hairpin turn and the abrasive action of the water has created a pronounced hook in the solid rock of the riverbank. The crag gets its name from Sir John Wintour (or Winter), a royalist officer who, while being chased by Parliamentarian forces during the English Civil War, is alleged to have ridden his horse over the edge of the precipice and swum across the river to safety.

CHEPSTOW

The triangle of land lying between the B4228 and the A48 to the east of here is known as **Tidenham Chase**. This 1000 acre area of open land once belonged to the lords of Chepstow who set it aside for deer hunting. In places, the underlying limestone breaks through the surface in a series of dramatic outcrops which make excellent viewpoints for surveying the surrounding landscape.

The River Wye reaches the Severn estuary near the ancient Gwent market town of Chepstow. This strategically important point was the location of the first Norman stone fortress in Wales. **Chepstow Castle** was extended several times over the centuries and it now occupies a substantial site on a limestone ridge above the Wye, which in turn forms a natural moat along its eastern side. During the 13th century, the tower which later became known as Martens Tower was added. This was where Henry

Marten, a co-signatory of Charles I's death warrant, was confined until his death in 1680. Chepstow Castle, with its lofty keep, defensive towers and sweeping courtyards, is open daily, 9.30am (2pm Sundays) to 6.30pm (4pm in winter), all year round.

The George Hotel enjoys a prime position at the top of Chepstow's High Street, adjoining the medieval port wall and the picturesque 16th century town gate. Originally constructed as an inn and posting house, this impressive family-style hotel has lost none of its historic character.

In recent years, it has been tastefully refurbished to provide all the modern facilities expected by patrons and guests from around the world. Its fourteen bedrooms are now luxuriously appointed and individually decorated. All the guest rooms are equipped with private bathrooms, televisions, radios, telephones and hot drinks facilities, whilst cots, highchairs and a baby-listening service are among the added benefits.

George Hotel, Moor Street, Chepstow Tel: 01291 625363
Fax: 01291 627418

Those with a taste for good food will find a varied and interesting menu in the Galleries Bistro, where a selection of international cuisine and local specialities is served in elegant surroundings. The experienced staff are friendly and attentive, and are certain to make your stay at The George a happy one.

A short distance away, **Chepstow Museum** houses a permanent exhibition on the history of this important port and military stronghold. Here, the commercial life of the town, which once included wine shipping, shipbuilding and salmon fishing, is brought to life in a series of imaginatively devised settings. Also on display is an interesting collection of 18th and 19th century prints portraying Chepstow, its castle and the countryside of the Wye Valley.

Bridge Inn, The Back, Chepstow Tel: 01291 625622

Situated by Chepstow's famous iron bridge, the **Bridge Inn** is a delightful old inn which was first recorded in 1687 when it was known as the Ship and Castle. Its main claim to fame is that in 1742, it was painted by the celebrated artist, William Turner. During the building of the iron bridge in 1815, the name of the pub was changed to its present one. Those stepping inside the Bridge today will be met by Byron and Jo, charming hosts who offer a warm welcome and superb food, including a choice of Welsh specialities. All meals are freshly made and there is plenty of choice. A wide range of traditional ales is offered, and the very pleasant atmosphere is further enhanced by a real log fire. The inn is beautifully situated on the banks of the River Wye which is reputed to have the second highest rise and fall in the world.

ALVINGTON

The main A48 to the northeast of Chepstow runs along the southern edge of Tidenham Chase. The churchyard in the pleasant village of Alvington, whose centre lies to the north of the main road, contains the graves of the Wintour family. As well as being known for Sir John Wintour's remarkable escape from Cromwell's forces at Wintour's Leap, this illustrious family played an important role in the defeat of the Spanish Armada over half-a-century before.

VINEY HILL

Situated at Viney Hill, just off the A48 between the Royal Forest of Dean and the River Severn, **Upper Viney Farmhouse** is owned and personally run as a bed and breakfast establishment by Mary and Malcolm Litten. Renowned for their warm hospitality, excellent home-cooking and comfortable accommodation, this is certainly one of the best places to stay in the area. As well as being the perfect holiday base, Upper Viney Farmhouse also has a very interesting past, one which Mary and Malcolm have investigated and are proud to recall.

Upper Viney Farmhouse, Viney Hill, Near Lydney
Tel: 01594 516672

Originally a small two bedroomed dwelling, the farmhouse was enlarged in the late 1700s, before a modern extension was added in the 1960s. Many artefacts have been uncovered during restoration and renovation work to the house, including a boot or shoe that dates from around 1800 which is thought to have been placed in a cavity in the remarkable spiral staircase to ward off ghosts. The building's internal walls are made of wattle and daub, and a section of this type of construction can be seen in the dining room. In fact, so many interesting items have been found on the site that Mary and Malcolm have their own mini museum which also contains Malcolm's collection of old farm implements.

LYDNEY

The famous **Lydney Park Gardens** lie beside the A48 on the western outskirts of Lydney. Today, these beautiful wooded grounds are filled with rhododendrons, azaleas, magnolias and other flowering shrubs which are at their best during May and early June. During the Second World War, however, the entire eight acre site was used for growing potatoes, and it wasn't until the second Lord Bledisloe and his head gardener, 'Mac' Stracey, set to work that the present landscape was created. This delightful woodland garden is only open for a short season each year, that is, on Sundays, Wednesdays and Bank Holidays between Easter and early-June, plus every day during the week of the Whitsun Bank Holiday. Telephone 01594 842844 to confirm opening times.

The grounds of Lydney Park also contain a number of features which form a fascinating record of human occupation in this part of the country. As well as the site of an Iron Age hill fort, there are the remains of a late Roman temple complex dating from the 4th century AD which was excavated by Sir Mortimer Wheeler in the 1920s. It is likely that the builders of this unusual temple were wealthy Romanised Celts, similar to those living at Chedworth or Great Witcombe. The building's mosaic floor, now sadly lost, depicted fish and sea monsters and was dedicated to the god Nodens, a Roman-Celtic god of healing whose emblem, in common with other early symbols of curing, was a reclining dog.

A collection of Roman artefacts from the site, including the famous 'Lydney Dog', are now housed in the nearby **Lydney Park Museum**. (Opening times similar to gardens.) In addition, the museum contains a number of interesting items which were brought back from New Zealand in the 1930s by the first Viscount Bledisloe following his term there as the Governor General. Lydney Park is populated by a herd of fallow deer and also contains evidence of Roman iron-mine workings and a line of earth fortifications of a similar age which were later reinforced by the Saxons.

Lydney itself is the largest settlement between Chepstow and Gloucester, occupies a site between the River Severn and the Forest of Dean. Those interested in the evocative world of steam railways should make a point of visiting the Norchard Steam Centre on the northern outskirts of the town. This is the headquarters of the **Dean Forest Railway** which was originally built in 1809 to haul coal and iron ore from the heart of the Forest of Dean to the docks on the Severn estuary. The line operated as a horse-drawn tramway until 1868 when it was updated to a broad gauge steam railway. Closed to passengers in 1929, British Rail continued to utilise the line for transporting coal and ballast until all services ceased in 1976.

The line then lay in a state of decay until the early 1980s, when the Dean Forest Railway Society acquired it and began a major programme of restoration. The first stage was completed in 1991 when a short stretch of track was reopened between Norchard and a new station at Lydney Lakeside, four miles to the south. Further work is currently in progress to reinstate the entire line between Lydney and Parkend, a project which will take many years to complete.

Norchard Steam Centre

Visitors to the **Norchard Steam Centre** can view the impressive collection of steam locomotives and rolling stock, several of which are still undergoing restoration. They can also visit the Society's railway museum with its unique display of signs, nameplates, posters, photographs and other railway items, including many from the local Severn and Wye line. There is also an on-site picnic area and a shop offering a wide variety of gifts and souvenirs.

On certain designated 'steam days', excursions are offered along the restored stretch of line. The eight mile return trip takes 35 minutes and includes a fifteen minute stop at Lydney Lakeside. Current steam days are all Sundays and Bank Holidays between April and September, plus Wednesdays in June and July, and Tuesdays, Wednesdays and Thursdays in August.

BREAM

Forest of Dean Gallery and Workshop, Blue Rock Crescent, Bream, Near Lydney Tel: 01594 562227

Situated in the former mining community of Bream, three miles to the northwest of Lydney, the **Forest of Dean Gallery and Craft Workshop** is a place not to be missed. Proprietor Phyllis Lewis is a ceramic sculptress well known in the Forest of Dean, and since appearing on national radio and television she has been able to spread the message about her gallery to a wider audience. Born in Bream in the mid 1930s, Phyllis is determined to keep alive the memories of that period with her unique exhibition of original sculptures. The exhibition is enhanced by photographs by David Lloyd depicting life in the mining community and the Forest of Dean.

The gallery and workshop provide a social history which celebrates the past and present times of the Forest, and in particular the brave men and women whose daily lives were so dictated by the hazardous conditions of mining. Visitors are welcome to view the wonderful sculptures, many of which are for sale, along with a range of top quality handmade gifts made by craftsmen and women living in the Forest which are offered at reasonable prices. Situated to the rear of Farmer and Clark in Blue Rock Crescent, the gallery and workshop are open daily, 10am to 4pm (closed 12.30pm to 1.30pm).

BLAKENEY

The attractive small village of Blakeney lies four miles along the A48 to the northeast of Lydney. At this point, drivers can join the Forestry Commission's 25 mile circular scenic drive through the central area of the Forest of Dean. The first stage of the journey leads up through the steep-sided Soudley Valley. Here, the road follows the twisting course of the river, resulting in a series of challenging gradients and bends.

BLACKPOOL BRIDGE

At Blackpool Bridge, the scenic drive crosses a recognisable section of the old Roman road which once ran between Lydney and Ariconium, near Ross-on-Wye. The bridge itself was constructed to replace a ford which crossed Blackpool Brook at this point.

LOWER SOUDLEY

Situated deep in the heart of the forest, the fascinating **Dean Heritage Centre** occupies a site at Camp Mill on the edge of Lower Soudley. During the 17th century there was a foundry here, then later, the buildings were modified to house a leatherboard mill where heel stiffeners and shoe insoles were manufactured. More recently, the site has been a saw mill and a piggery, then in 1981, it was presented to the Dean Heritage Museum Trust and within just two years, the first specialised displays of the new heritage centre were opened to the public.

The social history of the forest people is shown through domestic artefacts and documents which have been given to the museum by local inhabitants. As a result of their geographical isolation from both England

and Wales, the forest folk formed a fiercely independent society which developed its own customs, rights and even law courts, as well as a deep suspicion of outsiders.

Exhibits include a reconstructed miner's cottage containing a typical living room, bedroom and wash house of around 1900, a beam engine built by Samuel Hewlett around the turn of the 18th century, and a twelve foot overshot water wheel which has been constructed within the original wheel pit of the mill to emphasise the importance of water power in the industrial development of the area. Outside, there is a typical Forest smallholding complete with an orchard and Gloucester Old Spot pigs, a reconstructed cider press, and a traditional charcoal burner's hut. Several nature trails radiate from the centre, which also incorporates a number of craft workshops and the popular Heritage Kitchen.

After leaving the Dean Heritage Centre, the scenic drive soon passes the attractive small lakes known as the **Soudley Ponds**. Then, after passing the White Horse pub, it's worth making a short diversion onto the Littledean Road to visit the **Blaize Bailey** viewpoint. This can be reached by turning east after a mile or so onto a forest track. Once there, visitors are rewarded with breathtaking views over the village of Newnham and the Vale of Gloucester to the Cotswold Hills beyond. Another wonderful view, this time of Soudley village, can be obtained from a lay-by which is passed on the return to the scenic drive.

The next place to stop is the famous **Dean Sculpture Trail**, a unique collection of outdoor sculptures which are spaced along a delightful woodland walk. In each case, the artists have used the forest setting as their theme, for example, one piece known as the Cathedral is an impressive stained-glass window which depicts the trees, plants and wildlife of the forest. The sculpture trail is accessible either from the picnic area adjacent to the stained-glass window, or from the award-winning Beechenhurst picnic site a mile or so further west; both are sited on the northern side of the B4226.

Situated on the opposite side of the road at this point is the **Speech House Arboretum**, a fascinating place for those interested in the world of trees. Visitors can view the large collection of native and imported specimen trees which are laid out along a pleasant woodland trail. A little further west is the historic Speech House Hotel, the official meeting place of the ancient Verderers' Court.

Littledean Hall, Newnham

CANNOP

At nearby Cannop Crossroads, a sign points east to the **Cannop Ponds** picnic area. These picturesque pools were originally hollowed out in the 1820s to provide a regular water supply for the local iron smelting works.

Why not take a break from the car and go biking in the Cannop Valley? **Pedalabikeaway**, run by Fred Carpenter, has bikes of all sizes for all ages and levels of experience, including those with disabilities. Bikes can be hired by the hour, or there are daily and family rates. Fred can advise on routes and supply maps, books and refreshments. The cycle centre is open 10am to 5pm, every day during July, August and the school holidays; Tuesdays to Sundays between April and September; and weekends only between October and March.

Pedalabikeaway Cycle Centre, Cannop Valley, Forest of Dean
Tel: 01594 860065 and 01989 770357

NAGSHEAD

Continuing in an anticlockwise direction, the wildlife reserve at Nagshead near Parkend is worth a visit. The Forest of Dean has long been a haven for a huge variety of animals and birds, including deer, badgers, woodpeckers and the famous forest sheep which have been allowed to range freely in the forest for centuries. The **Nagshead Reserve** is particularly noted for its resident population of pied flycatchers and visiting peregrine falcons.

PARKEND

The attractive former mineral extracting community of Parkend stands at the northern terminus of the still to be completed Dean Forest Railway. Not far from here, the charmingly named **New Fancy View** is a delightfully landscaped picnic area which was once the site the New Fancy Colliery. It's worth making the effort to climb to the summit of the nearby hill for a breathtaking view over the forest landscape.

Half-a-mile after returning to the main circuit, a detour to the north leads to the beautiful **Mallards Pike Lake**, another good place for a short walk. For those wishing to press on, the track follows a circular route back onto the scenic drive. The final place worth mentioning is the **Wenchford** picnic site in the central area of the fores. This is situated a mile further east and can be reached by turning north onto the Soudley road and then immediately east onto an old railway track leading to a parking area (toilets are available here).

NEWNHAM

Having returned to the A48 at Blakeney, the pleasant community of Newnham lies three miles to the northeast. This is considered to be one of the best places for viewing the famous **Severn Bore**, the natural wave created when the incoming tide from the Bristol Channel is channelled into the narrow Severn estuary. Although small-scale bores occur throughout the year, certain tidal conditions cause a wave of some nine feet in height to be generated, usually on the spring tides of early spring or late autumn. The phenomenon is popular with surfers and canoeists who attempt to 'catch the wave'. Information on the best viewing times and places can be obtained from local retailers.

Littledean Hall lies a mile-and-a-half up a steep lane to the northwest of Newnham. Surrounded by sweeping grounds, this magnificent country house occupies a dramatic position overlooking the great horseshoe bend on the Severn. (It lies only a short distance from Blaize Bailey viewpoint mentioned on the scenic drive around the central area of the Forest of Dean). A house with a long and rich history, Littledean Hall is one of the oldest continuously occupied country residences in England. In 1984, the remains of **Springhead Temple**, one of the largest Roman shrines in rural Britain, were discovered in the foundations, and there is also evidence of a great hall dating from Saxon times. The Norman core of the present day house was built for the Dene family in the 11th century, then a new Jacobean building was added in 1612. Some exceptional carved wood panelling from this era is still much in evidence throughout the interior, along with a variety of features relating to the further alterations which were made between 1664 and 1896.

Littledean Hall's main claim to fame, however, is its many ghosts, the majority of which seem to have their origins in the period since the 17th century. One of the earliest recorded apparitions dates from the English Civil War when the hall's royalist garrison was surprised by a Parliamentarian attack. After the royalists surrendered, one of the their troops unfortunately killed one of the Roundhead soldiers, an act which resulted in the entire garrison being massacred. Royalist colonels Congreve and Wigmore were standing next to the main fireplace when they were put to the sword and today, phantom bloodstains are said to appear at the spot which no amount of cleaning can remove.

Another event which is said to account for some of the present poltergeist activity took place a century later in 1744. According to legend, the then owner of the house, Charles Pyrke, was murdered by his black manservant, despite the two having been friends since childhood. (Pyrke was alleged to have been responsible for making his servant's sister pregnant and subsequently murdering the baby.) Today, the ghostly butler is said to haunt the landing outside his former garret bedroom high in the east wing.

Some years later, the Pyrke family were again involved in a murderous incident when two brothers in love with the same woman ended up killing each other during an argument at the dining table. According to legend, their spirits still inhabit the dining room. One unfortunate result of all this poltergeist activity is that one of the best guest rooms, the Blue Room, is believed to be so disturbed by the sound of footsteps and the clashing of swords that no one has dared to spend a night in the room for over 40 years. Littledean Hall is open daily, 10.30am to 6pm between April and October.

WESTBURY-UPON-SEVERN

Leaving the haunted garrets and passageways behind, the pleasant community of Westbury-upon-Severn, a couple of miles to the east, is home to the National Trust-owned **Westbury Court Garden**. This unique open space was built between 1696 and 1705, making it the earliest surviving example of a formal Dutch water garden in the country. When the Trust acquired the property in the 1960s, it was in a state of serious dilapidation: the house had been demolished, the water courses had silted up, the garden walls were crumbling and the lawns were like hayfields.

However, with the help of an engraving of the original garden plan, records of the initial plantings and a series of special grants, the Trust was able to begin a programme of restoration which was finally completed in 1971.

Today, Westbury Court Garden provides an opportunity to experience at first hand the style of formal landscaping which existed before the onset of emparking later in the 18th century. The only building to survive is an elegant two-storey redbrick pavilion with a tower and weather vane which stands overlooking the garden's delightful waterlily-filled canals. Another particularly appealing feature of this most attractive and interesting garden is that it was exclusively replanted with species known to have been available in this part of the country before 1700. (Open Wednesdays to Sundays and Bank Holiday Mondays, 11am to 6pm between April and end October.)

CHAPTER TWO
South Gloucestershire

Dyrham Park

Avon Valley Railway

2
South Gloucestershire

THORNBURY

The bustling market town of Thornbury lies between the River Severn and the M5, in the part of southern Gloucestershire which used to fall within the county of Avon. A prosperous dormitory settlement with many recent housing developments, its old centre still possesses a surprising number of Georgian and earlier buildings. The original main streets of the Plane, the High Street and Castle Street form a characteristic medieval 'Y' pattern which converges on the old marketplace, now a frequent bottleneck. Not far away, two giant creatures, a lion and a swan, stare out at each other across the High Street from their positions above the main entrances to the White Lion and Swan hotels, two handsome former coaching inns which have been rivals since the 18th century. Thornbury also has a number of prominent Victorian buildings which display a curious mixture of architectural styles. These include a neo-Renaissance bank, a neo-Gothic Methodist chapel, a neo-Gothic street fountain, and the registry office of 1839 which has an Egyptian doorway, Doric pilasters and a Georgian pediment.

Thornbury was an important producer of woollen cloth during the late medieval era and the town's surprisingly large parish **Church** reflects this early period of prosperity. A largely 14th century Perpendicular building which incorporates parts of an earlier Norman structure, it is set away from the main centre near the site of the old manor house. The church has an impressive tower and a side chapel dedicated to the Stafford family, the local lords of the manor whose family emblem, the Stafford Knot, is much in evidence.

Edward Stafford, the third Duke of Buckingham, was responsible for starting work on the adjacent **Thornbury Castle** in 1511. Sadly, he wasn't able to see the project through to completion for in 1522, he was charged with high treason by Henry VIII and beheaded on London's Tower Hill. Part-castle, part-country mansion, the building was eventually completed in the 1850s by Anthony Salvin. It is now run as a first-class restaurant and is not open to the general public; however, a good view of the exterior can be had from the north side of the churchyard.

Thornbury Castle

OLDBURY-UPON-SEVERN

The attractive former salmon-fishing village of Oldbury-upon-Severn is situated to the northwest of Thornbury between two great monuments to 1960s technology: the Severn suspension bridge and the Oldbury nuclear power station. Despite its name, the settlement lies more than half-a-mile from the riverbank, an indication that the flat strip of land along the estuary was once subject to severe flooding. The parish **Church** stands in a striking position on top of a small hill some distance from the village. According to local legend, all attempts to build the church closer to the centre were foiled by a mysterious nocturnal force which repeatedly dismantled the newly constructed walls: each morning the stonemasons would arrive to discover their previous day's work had been torn to the ground.

Eventually, a local sage prescribed that two maiden heifers should be released in the parish and the church constructed on the spot they chose to graze. As a result, the rise on which the building now stands is known as Cowhill. The church is dedicated to the martyred St Arilda, a virgin who was beheaded at nearby Kington because she refused to surrender her honour to an evil local baron. The original Norman spire collapsed in a storm in 1703, and much of the remainder of the building was destroyed by fire in 1897. As a consequence, the present structure is largely late Victorian, although it still contains some interesting 17th and 18th century monuments and table tombs. There is a magnificent view from the churchyard across the Severn estuary to Chepstow and the Forest of Dean.

SHEPPERDINE

The local inn in the hamlet of Shepperdine, two miles to the north, is named after a traditional mariners' excuse. Severn bargees having one too many in the pub formed the habit of blaming their unwillingness to put to sea on the local weather conditions. The practice of telling their employers they were 'windbound' eventually became so widespread that the pub's name was changed from the New Inn to the Windbound. Despite its close proximity to a high sea wall, the combined of effects of strong winds and an exceptionally high tide can occasionally cause seawater to blow onto the roof and down the chimneys.

AUST

The English end of the original **Severn Suspension Bridge** lies three miles to the southwest of Oldbury-upon-Severn at Aust. Completed in 1966 at a cost of £8 million, this elegant toll bridge replaced the ferry which, in various forms, had plied back and forth across this treacherous stretch of water since Roman times. The bridge carries the busy M4 across the mouth of Britain's longest river to South Wales.

SEVERN BEACH

However, the Suspension Bridge's susceptibility to high winds, coupled with its inability to carry peak volumes of traffic, recently necessitated the construction of a **Second Severn Crossing**, three miles downstream at Severn Beach, a small resort and dormitory town which developed in the 1920s as a destination for day-trippers from Bristol. The Severn rail tunnel also passes under the estuary at this point. The area around the mouth of the River Avon to the southwest of Severn Beach should generally be avoided by the casual visitor.

ALMONDSBURY

The sprawling community of Almondsbury lies four miles to the east of Severn Beach beside the old ridgeway route from Bristol to Gloucester, now the A38. Despite some heavy-handed restoration by the Victorians, the medieval parish **Church of St Mary** retains some of its original features, including the Norman font and doorway in the north porch. It also has a rare lead-covered broach spire, one of only three in southern England, and a number of fine windows, including one which serves as a memorial to Charles Richardson, the 19th century engineer who designed and built the Severn tunnel. The parish is said to be frequented by ghosts: the ruins of the Elizabethan mansion, Over Court, are visited by a mysterious white lady, and the local inn, the Blue Bowl, is haunted by the ghost of a six year old French girl, Elizabeth Maronne, who can sometimes be heard reciting nursery rhymes in her native tongue.

The most curious event in Almondsbury's history took place in 1817 at nearby Knole Park when a young woman turned up at the local squire's door insisting she was a kidnapped oriental princess who had escaped from her captors by jumping overboard from their ship as it sailed up the Bristol Channel. Claiming she was unable to speak English, and abetted by a Portuguese sailor who maintained he understood her, she managed to convince the squire and his family that she was the Princess Caraboo. She was duly taken in, and within weeks, she was being wined and dined by fashionable Bath society. Unfortunately, her notoriety eventually came to the attention of her former Bristol landlady who exposed her as Mary Baker, a penniless woman from Devon. To save further embarrassment, her hosts raised enough money to buy her a one-way ticket to Philadelphia, but she returned to Bristol some years later and lived there until her death in 1865.

TOCKINGTON

Situated two miles to the northeast of Almondsbury, **Oldown House** is a small open farm and kitchen garden which lies off the A38 near the village of Tockington. Visitors can meet the shire horse and other farmyard animals, feed the lambs, ride on a trailer, walk in the woods or try their hand at the forest challenge. There is also an interesting interpretation centre, a licensed restaurant, and a charming Victorian kitchen garden with its own shop selling produce from this and other farms. Pick-you-own fruit and vegetables are also available in season. (Open daily except non-Bank Holiday Mondays, 10am to 6pm between Easter and end October.)

TORTWORTH

The roads to the northeast of Thornbury lead over the M5 at junction 14 to the former estate village of Tortworth. This attractive community is arranged around a broad green which is overlooked by **St Leonard's Church**, a part 14th century building which was substantially remodelled by the Victorians. Inside, there are some fine 15th century stained-glass windows and an unusual pair of canopied tombs belonging to the Throckmorton family, former owners of the Tortworth Park estate. The famous **Tortworth Chestnut** can be seen in a field near the church. This massive Spanish chestnut was described by the 17th century diarist, John Evelyn, as 'the great chestnut of King Stephen's time'. The tree was already believed to be over 600 years old when a fence was put up to protect it in 1800. A brass plaque was erected at the same time which was inscribed with the verse:

> *'May man still guard thy venerable form*
> *From the rude blasts and tempestuous storms.*
> *Still mayest thou flourish through succeeding time*
> *And last long last the wonder of the clime.'*

Over the centuries, the tree's twisted lower limbs have bent to the ground and rooted, or *layered*, in the soil, creating the impression of a small copse. Its appearance is particularly enchanting in early spring when the ground beneath is carpeted in wild snowdrops.

CHARFIELD

One-and-a-half miles to the southeast of Tortworth, the village of Charfield stands beside the main Bristol to Birmingham railway line. The old parish churchyard, which lies to the south of the village at Churchend, contains the common grave of fourteen unfortunate victims of a railway accident which took place near here early one morning in 1928. The disaster happened in thick fog when a freight train failed to clear the main line in time. A passenger express travelling at full speed smashed into the goods train, and the force of the collision piled the carriages against the road bridge in Charfield. To make matters worse, a second freight train travelling in the opposite direction collided with the first, causing a consignment of gas canisters to explode and setting the wreckage on fire. Of the fourteen casualties, two were thought to be children, although they may have been jockeys as some were known to have been on the train. Strangely, the two small bodies were never claimed by their relatives, although for years after a mysterious woman dressed in black was seen from time to time kneeling by their memorial in the churchyard. The identity of all three remains a mystery to this day.

WICKWAR

A couple of miles to the south, the B4060 passes through Wickwar, a tranquil backwater which was once a prosperous market town and wool centre. Despite the fact that its population rarely exceeded 1000, Wickwar used to elect its own mayor and corporation, and at one time, it could boast two breweries. In the 1890s, it was one of the first towns in the west of England to install electric street lighting, earlier even than Bristol. The curious round tower near the church stands above a vertical shaft which was built in 1841 to ventilate the half-mile-long railway tunnel which runs beneath the village. The **Church** itself is a Victorian rebuild, except for the tower which survives from the original 15th century structure. The interior contains an unusual medieval sculpture of St John the Baptist which came from Pool House, the now demolished Tudor manor house which once stood in parkland to the southwest.

Elsewhere in Wickwar, there are an unusual number of elegant Georgian buildings, including the late 18th century town hall with its distinctive bell tower and arches. The old grammar school and schoolmaster's house in the main street were built in the 1680s by Alexander Hosea, a wealthy Dick Whittington-like character who, at the age of fourteen, ran away to London to make his fortune.

A minor road to the east of Wickwar leads across the delightfully named stretch of open countryside known as South Moon Ridings and on up to the Cotswold ridge. The **Hawkesbury Monument** stands in a dramatic position on the crest of the hill. Designed by Vulliamy in unusual Chinese style, it was erected in 1846 as a memorial to Lord Robert Somerset of nearby Badminton, an army general who fought at Waterloo. Those climbing the 145 steps to the top are rewarded with magnificent views along the Cotswold escarpment to the north and south, and across the River Severn to the Welsh mountains to the west.

HAWKESBURY

This village is divided into two parts, one at the foot, and the other at the top of the Cotswold ridge. The surprisingly grand parish **Church of St Mary the Virgin** stands in the lower part surrounded only by the old parsonage and a small collection of farm buildings. Built in a succession of Norman and Gothic styles, the scale of the church reflects an earlier time of prosperity when this large rural parish was a thriving producer of woollen cloth. A charming notice near the Norman south doorway pronounces: 'It is desired that all persons that come to this church would be careful to leave their dogs at home and that the women would not walk in with their pattens on.' (Pattens were a type of wooden clog with a raised metal under-sole which kept the wearer's feet clear of the mud.) A rare example of this antique footwear still hangs nearby.

The church also contains a number of impressive monuments to the Jenkins family, the earls of Liverpool. Nearby Hawkesbury Manor, their now demolished family home, was the setting for a tragic 17th century story of forbidden love when the daughter of Protestant Sir Robert Jenkins fell in love with a member of the Catholic Paston family of Horton Manor. The couple were forced to part, and as her lover rode away, the young Miss Jenkins waved her final farewell from a top floor window and toppled to her death. The other part of the village, **Hawkesbury Upton**, stands on the ridge above. A typical Cotswold settlement which can seem grey and windswept in bad weather, it transforms into an idyllic community of neat stone cottages and country inns when the sun shines.

HORTON

The long ribbon-like village of Horton lies a couple of miles south of Hawkesbury church at the foot of the Cotswold escarpment. The National Trust-owned **Horton Court** can be found on higher ground to the northeast of the village. This part-Norman Cotswold-stone manor house was rebuilt for William Knight, the royal ambassador who was given the task of presenting Henry VIII's case to the Pope when the King was endeavouring to divorce Catherine of Aragon. The building contains many quirky Renaissance features which were inspired by the ambassador's travels in Europe. One of the finest, a covered walkway, or ambulatory, which is detached from the main house, is thought to have been modelled on a Roman cloister.

Prior to its Tudor rebuilding, Horton Court had been the official residence of a prosperous ecclesiastical estate which had been founded in Norman times. The remarkable early 12th century great hall survives from this period, although a number of alterations, including the addition of windows and a dividing floor, have been made in the ensuing centuries. In 1884, the hall was restored to something resembling its original state, and it and the ambulatory are open to the public on Wednesdays and Saturdays, 2pm to 6pm between late March and end October. The attractive little **Church of St James** stands next to Horton Court. Heavily restored in 1865, it was built between the 14th and 16th centuries and still retains many of its original features. Inside, there is a restored Norman font and a number of memorials to the Paston family, the local lords of the manor during the Jacobean period. Together, the church, manor house and nearby farmstead create a quintessentially English scene.

LITTLE SODBURY

One-and-a-half miles to the south of Horton, the attractive hamlet of Little Sodbury stands on a slope below the great Iron Age hill fort from which it takes its name. The church, the only one in Britain dedicated to St Adeline, was built in Victorian times to replace one which was situated further up the hill near **Little Sodbury Manor**. This privately owned manor house was built in Tudor times for Sir John Walshe. Henry VIII and Anne Boleyn are reputed to have stayed here whilst en route to Bristol in 1535. Despite being extensively remodelled in Elizabethan times and again in 1919, the 15th century great hall, with its impressive open-timbered roof, remains. William Tyndale, the first scholar to translate the New Testament into English, served as a chaplain and tutor to the Walshe family during the 1520s. (See Chapter 5, North Nibley.) In 1556, Little Sodbury Manor was hit by a massive lighting strike; the bolt killed one boy outright, and seven other people died from shock within the next two months.

OLD SODBURY

Standing on a loop off the busy A432, Little Sodbury's sister village of Old Sodbury is situated on the opposite side of the Iron Age hill fort, one mile to the south. Despite some intrusive modern residential development, the village is worth visiting for its fine part-Norman church. This contains some exceptional tombs and monuments, including a carved stone effigy of a 13th century knight who is almost hidden behind his shield, a wooden effigy of a knight carved at Bristol in the late 14th century which is one of only five still in existence, and the tomb of David Harley, the Georgian diplomat who negotiated the treaty which ended the American War of Independence.

Old Sodbury church stands on a raised mound above the village, a place which offers some dramatic views over the surrounding landscape. The curious castellated tower to the east of here stands above a vertical shaft, one of a series built to ventilate the two-and-a-half mile long railway tunnel which carries the main London-South Wales line through the Cotswold escarpment. Opened in 1903, the tunnel required its own brick-making works and took over five years to complete.

A lane to the south of Old Sodbury leads to **Dodington House**, another in the string of country mansions lying along the base of the escarpment. The 700 acre Dodington estate was acquired in the 16th century by the Codrington family after its previous owner had exhausted all his funds attempting to build one of the most extravagant stately homes in the country. A century-and-a-half later, Capability Brown was brought in to landscape the grounds, and his inspired designs are responsible for the bold vistas, lakes and the small castellated Gothic structure now known as the Cascade Building.

Intended to be one of the great houses of its day, the present Dodington House was built between 1796 and 1816 on the site of an Elizabethan predecessor. It was designed with three front elevations in lavish neo-Roman style by the celebrated classical architect, James Wyatt. (Sadly, he wasn't able to see his work through to completion as he was killed in a carriage accident in 1813.) The exterior is a satisfying mixture of pilasters, pediments and porticos, although the interior, with its overabundance of gilt, marble and brass, may be considered a little overblown by present day standards. An elegant curved conservatory connects the house to the little private church of St Mary, another Wyatt creation designed in the shape of a Greek cross. Now open to visitors, Dodington House offers a variety of attractions, including a carriage collection in the stables, an adventure playground, and an exhibition of early maps, deeds and architectural plans. (Open daily, 11am to 6pm between Easter and end September.)

BADMINTON

The famous 15000 acre **Badminton Park** estate lies a couple of miles from the eastern end of the railway tunnel. Indeed, Badminton once had its own main line station, which was actually situated in the village of Acton Turville. The estate was founded by Edward Somerset, the canny son of the Marquis of Worcester who denounced Catholicism after his father had spent most of his vast family fortune supporting the doomed Royalist cause of Charles I. Instead, he allied himself to the Protestant Oliver Cromwell, but then a few years later, he championed the restoration of Charles II and was created the Duke of Beaufort for his pains. His striking 25 foot monument can be seen in the little church which adjoins the main house. This was originally installed in St George's chapel, Windsor, but was removed to make room for a memorial to Queen Victoria's father.

The central section of **Badminton House** dates from the 1680s and contains some exquisite lime-wood carving by Grinling Gibbons. The remainder was designed in the mid 18th century by William Kent, an architect of the Palladian school who was also responsible for landscaping the grounds and erecting the many impressive follies and gateways which litter the estate. The house also contains an impressive collection of art, including paintings from the Italian, English and Dutch schools.

A former Duke of Beaufort and his guests are reputed to have devised the game of badminton during a weekend party in the 1860s. The assembled company wanted to play indoor tennis in the entrance hall, but were concerned they may damage the paintings on the walls. Then someone came up with the idea of using a cork studded with feathers in place of a ball and the rest, as they say, is history. A few years later, one of the guests is believed to have taken a version of the game to the Indian subcontinent where the first formal rules were drawn up in Karachi in 1877.

Many of the buildings on the Badminton estate, including the parish **Church of St Michael and All Angels** which stands adjacent to the main house, were designed in romantic castellated style by the architect Thomas Wright. Examples of his architectural influence can also be seen in the two estate villages of **Great** and **Little Badminton**. The former contains a handsome row of early 18th century almshouses which bear the name of their benefactor, the Beauforts, and the latter is set around an attractive village green which has a medieval dovecote at its centre and is overlooked by a small part 13th century church. Each year in April, the park is the venue for the famous **Badminton Horse Trials**, an international three-day event which attracts participants and spectators from all over the world.

CHIPPING SODBURY

Returning to the base of the Cotswold ridge, the pleasant former market town of Chipping Sodbury lies on the A432, five miles west of Badminton. One of the earliest examples of town planning in Britain, the settlement was laid out in narrow strips on either side of the broad main street in the 12th century. Although the market has long since disappeared, the main street, which is wide enough for cars to park end-on, remains an attractive thoroughfare of 17th to 19th century buildings whose contrasting styles and materials combine to form a delightful whole.

Sultan Restaurant, Melbourne House, 29 Horse Street, Chipping Sodbury Tel: 01454 323510

A unique restaurant which combines the exotic flavours of Indian cuisine with the elegance of a Georgian town house can be found at the eastern end of Chipping Sodbury town centre. The popular and much-recommended **Sultan Restaurant** has occupied Melbourne House in Horse Street since 1983. The former home of Dr Edward Jenner, the father of medical vaccination, its handsome Georgian façade was built onto an earlier structure dating from 1664.

Now converted to a modern restaurant, the Sultan is owned and personally run by Masood and Manju Haque, charming hosts who provide a warm welcome, excellent service and some of the finest cuisine in the area. The extensive menu contains a wide range of familiar and more adventurous dishes from the Indian subcontinent, including tandoori specialities, vegetarian dishes and popular baltis. (The Murg Tikka Rezala, a fairly hot, sweet and sour dish, is truly delicious.) In its time, the Sultan has been awarded a place in the AA's top 500 restaurants in Britain, the only Indian restaurant in the West Country to receive this accolade. Open seven evenings a week, it is worth travelling a long way to enjoy fine Indian cooking in this unique Georgian setting.

Chipping Sodbury's unusually large part 13th century **Church** was constructed during the medieval period of prosperity when the town was a thriving weaving and market centre. After a long period of decline, the second half of the 20th century has seen some rapid development, both in Chipping Sodbury and nearby Yate, communities which have been virtually united by a series of modern housing estates which were thrown up to cope with the population overspill from Bristol and Bath.

TORMARTON

Lying on the eastern side of the A46 a mile-and-a-half from Dodington, the **Portcullis Inn** at Tormarton is conveniently situated within easy reach of junction 18 on the M4.

Portcullis Inn, Tormarton Tel: 01454 218263

The exterior of this imposing 350 year old Cotswold stone inn is clothed in ivy and creeper, creating a spectacular blaze of greens and reds. The inn features prominently on the local tithe map of 1849, whilst the nearby village church is listed in the Domesday Book. Recommended for its good food, the Portcullis is very popular with those in the know. The restaurant menu offers a wide choice, and there is a very pleasant atmosphere in the bar, where eight beers are served from the cask, along with lagers, bottled beers, wines and spirits. The inn also offers first-rate accommodation in seven en-suite guest bedrooms. With its quiet unspoilt village setting, this is an ideal place to stay and relax. There is also a function room which is equipped for conferences and business seminars for up to forty delegates.

Dyrham Park

The A46 to the south of Tormarton crosses the M4 then passes close to the site of a momentous battle which took place between the Saxons and the Britons in the 6th century. According to the Anglo-Saxon Chronicle, three British kings were killed in the encounter which paved the way for the Saxon occupation of western England.

The National Trust-owned **Dyrham Park** stands on the slope of the Cotswold ridge, half-a-mile to the south of the battlefield. Recognisable to some as the setting for *The Remains Of The Day*, the award winning film starring Anthony Hopkins and Emma Thompson, this striking baroque mansion was built at the turn of the 18th century for William Blathwayt, a career civil servant and diplomat who rose to become Secretary of State to William III.

Despite its appearance of unity, the building was constructed in two separate phases. The first, which includes the west front facing down the valley, was completed around 1696 to a design by the Huguenot Samuel Hauduroy and the second, which includes the stable-block, orangery and elegant many-windowed east front, was completed around 1710 to a design by William Talman, a deputy of Sir Christopher Wren. The largely unaltered interior houses a wonderful collection of fixtures and artefacts accumulated by the original owner during his postings to Holland and North America. These include a number of rare Dutch paintings and a magnificent collection of blue and white Delft porcelain. The strong connection with the Netherlands was recently acknowledged in the naming of a new variety of Dutch flame tulip, 'Dyrham Park'. (Open daily except Wednesdays and Thursdays, 12 noon to 5.30pm between late March and end October.)

The west front of Dyrham Park looks out across a delightful terrace to the lawned gardens beyond. These were laid out in formal Dutch style until the end of the 18th century when the fashion for sweeping tracts of parkland came in and supplanted the earlier formality. Much of the 263 acre estate is now stocked with fallow deer, an apparent reversion to its ancient use as the name Dyrham means 'deer enclosure' in Saxon. A charming little church stands on a terrace overlooking the garden a few yards from the house. A largely 15th- century structure with 13th century parts, it contains a Norman font, a fine 15th century monumental brass, and a number of impressive memorials to members of the Wynter and Blathwayt families.

MARSHFIELD

Three miles to the southeast of Dyrham Park, the A420 skirts around the old market town of Marshfield. Although it is hard to imagine today, this was once the fourth wealthiest town in Gloucestershire after Bristol, Gloucester and Cirencester. Its once thriving malt and wool industries have long since disappeared and it is now little more than a village. However, Marshfield still possesses an unusually long and interesting

High Street which is lined with handsome buildings dating from the 17th and 18th centuries, a period when the town was an important stop on the main coaching route between Bristol and London. In its heyday, there were over a dozen coaching inns in this street, including the famous Catherine Wheel, one of only three that remain today. Another relic from the era of the stagecoach is an 18th century road sign bearing the inscription, '103 miles to London, 12 miles and 1 furlong to Bristol'.

Much of the old part of Marshfield, between the 17th century Elias Crispe almshouses at one end of the High Street and the imposing parish Church of St Mary at the other, has now been designated a conversation area. Among of the many noteworthy structures to be seen here are the Tolzey market hall of 1690 which was rebuilt in 1793, and a pair of early 18th century coaching inns, both of which have curious shell-hooded doorways. The church contains a fine Jacobean pulpit and some impressive 17th and 18th century monuments.

One of the Cotswolds' more eccentric businesses operated in the High Street until 1983. Bodman's Grocery and Drapery Shop was founded by Mr Bodman Sr in 1860s, and when it eventually passed to Mr Bodman Jr, his son made so few alterations that the store gradually became a living museum. Young Mr Bodman left the Edwardian fixtures and fittings intact, and if a long-standing item of stock took his fancy, he would often refuse to sell it. This situation persisted until his death at the age of 90, when the contents of the shop were snapped up by a grateful horde of museum curators and antique dealers.

Each year on Boxing Day the town is taken over by the **Marshfield Mummers**, a troupe of players who perform a unique piece of street theatre whose origins go back to pagan times. Based on the ancient themes of fertility and good versus evil, this unique celebration was revived in the 1930s by the local vicar after an interval of over 50 years. The characters go by such colourful names as 'Doctor Phoenix', 'Saucy Jack' and 'King William - a Man of Courage and Bold', and the action includes a number of time-honoured set pieces, such as the death of winter and the rebirth of spring. The performers wear wonderful shaggy costumes made from strips of newspaper and are accompanied around the streets by a town crier wearing a top hat with a bright yellow band.

An interesting folk museum can be found on the northern edge of Marshfield at **Castle Farm**, a working farm which is open to the public during the summer months.

ST CATHERINE'S

To the south of Marshfield, a twisting lane leads through a delightful valley to this scattered hamlet. A surprisingly tranquil place without any real centre, it was once a monastic village and still displays the classic medieval triad of manor house, church and tithe barn. The Church contains an impressive 15th century stained-glass window, the four lights of which depict the Virgin Mary, the Crucifixion, St John and St Peter. The privately owned great manor house, **St Catherine's Court**, is a former monastic grange which once belonged to the Benedictine priory at Bath. The north front is genuine 16th century, although much of the rest of the building is a mock-Tudor imitation dating from the 19th century. The landscape around St Catherine's is exceptionally pleasant and offers some excellent walking.

LANGRIDGE

The attractive village of Langridge is situated on the opposite side of the A46, two miles to the west. A lane leads up from here onto the top of Lansdown, the site of the famous English Civil War battle of 1643. Despite the encounter ending in a Parliamentarian withdrawal, the Royalist commander, Sir Bevil Grenville, was mortally wounded and died later at the rectory in nearby Cold Ashton. A monument erected in 1720 stands at the place he is believed to have fallen. A mile-and-a-half to the south, flat races are held throughout the summer season at **Bath Racecourse** on the southern edge of Lansdown.

BITTON

The **Avon Valley Railway** operates from the old station at Bitton, midway between Bath and Bristol. When it originally opened in 1869, the line formed part of the Bath to Mangotsfield section of the Midland Railway. It continued to see healthy traffic until the 1950s when the increased use of motor transport led to a decline in passengers, a trend which eventually led to the closure of the line in 1972.

The first attempts at regeneration came from the Bristol Suburban Railway Society, the forerunner of the Avon Valley Railway, who took over Bitton Station which was then in very poor condition. With a workforce of volunteers, they rebuilt the station, re-laid the track and restored a number of locomotives and carriages so that trains could once again run to Oldland Common.

In August 1994, a new section of the southern extension was opened, completing the first in a three-stage plan to extend the line, firstly as far as the River Avon, and eventually to the outskirts of Bath, a total of five-and-a-half miles. A wonderful attraction for anyone with an interest in the age of steam, all entrance fees and profits from the sale of souvenirs are re-invested in the railway.

Avon Valley Railway

CHAPTER THREE
Vale of Berkeley to Tetbury

Chavenage Manor

The Great Hall, Berkeley Castle

3
Vale of Berkeley to Tetbury

BERKELEY

The low-lying **Vale of Berkeley** is bounded to the north by the River Severn and to the south by the M5. This fertile coastal strip takes its name from the peaceful little town of Berkeley, an ancient settlement with a largely Georgian centre which is dominated by its imposing Norman castle. Said to be the oldest castle in England still to be inhabited, it was built between 1117 and 1153 on the site of a Saxon fort and has remained in the Berkeley family for over 800 years.

Berkeley Castle

It was here that, in 1215, the barons of the West congregated before setting out to witness the sealing of the Magna Carta by King John at Runnymede. The incident which gave **Berkeley Castle** its greatest notoriety, however, was the gruesome murder of King Edward II in 1327. Years of ineffectual rule, made worse by his ill-judged choice of friends, led to Edward being usurped from the throne by his wife and her lover. He was imprisoned at Berkeley for several months, before being made to suffer a literally terrible end by way of 'a hoot brooche put into the secret place posteriale'. Subsequent monarchs appear to have received rather better treatment when visiting the castle. Richard II was well-entertained here and Elizabeth I is known to have stayed on a number of occasions.

Over the centuries Berkeley Castle has been magnificently maintained by the various Lords and Earls of Berkeley. Now open to the public, visitors enter this impressive stronghold by way of a bridge over a moat. Among the many things to see inside are the 14th century great hall, circular keep, state apartments with their fine tapestries and period furniture, medieval kitchens, and the actual dungeon where Edward II met his sticky end.

The castle is surrounded by an Elizabethan terraced garden which contains a number of interesting features, including a medieval bowling alley and a beautiful lily pond which was formerly a swimming pool. The grounds also incorporate a free-flight butterfly house, gift shop, tearoom and a large well-stocked deer park. (Open daily, except non-Bank Holiday Mondays, between April and September, plus Sunday afternoons during October.)

Memorials to several members of the Berkeley family can be seen in the parish **Church of St Mary**. This impressive building also has a fine Norman doorway, a detached tower which was added in 1783, and a striking east window with nine lights depicting scenes of Christ healing the sick. The churchyard contains the grave of pioneer immunologist Edward Jenner (1749-1823), who spent much of his life in the town.

The son of a local parson, Jenner was apprenticed to a surgeon in Chipping Sodbury in 1763 at the age of fourteen. Seven years later he moved to London to become a student at St George's Hospital, studying under the great surgeon John Hunter, before eventually returning to Berkeley to practice as a country doctor and to continue his pioneering work in immunology.

While still an apprentice, Jenner had become aware of the link between cowpox and smallpox, noticing that exposure to one protected against infection from the other. His work over several decades led to the first vaccination against smallpox, a disease which is thought to have killed as many as 60 million people worldwide in the preceding century. Thanks to Jenner's pioneering work, the disease has now been effectively been eradicated from the planet.

Jenner Museum, Berkeley

Jenner's former home, a splendid Georgian house in Church Lane known as the Chantry, was purchased in the early 1980s by a trust who converted it into the **Jenner Museum and Immunology Conference Centre**, thanks in part to a donation from the Japanese philanthropist Ryoichi Sasakawa. A thatched rustic hut where Jenner used to vaccinate the poor free of charge and which he named the 'Temple of Vaccinia' still stands in the grounds. (Museum open Tuesdays to Sundays between April and September.)

SLIMBRIDGE

The long rambling village of Slimbridge lies four miles to the northeast of Berkeley, off the A38 Gloucester road. The village has a fine 13th century church with large 18th century windows which incorporate fragments of original medieval glass. The main attraction here, however, is the world famous **Slimbridge Wildfowl and Wetlands Centre** which was founded in 1946 by Sir Peter Scott, the artist and naturalist son of Antarctic explorer, Captain Robert Falcon Scott.

Black Swans at Slimbridge

The centre provides sanctuary for many thousands of waterfowl, including some which remain here all year round and others which drop in on their spring and autumn migrations. Up to 3000 birds can be in residence at any one time, making Slimbridge one of the largest wildfowl reserves in the world. The Slimbridge Wildfowl and Wetlands Trust, whose headquarters are based here, have established seven other centres in the UK which together provide a home to over 200 different species of wetland birds.

Slimbridge's 73 acres of landscaped pens, lakes and paddocks stretch down to the River Severn and are open to visitors all year round. Numerous duck, goose, swan and other wildfowl species can be viewed at close quarters, and there are even hides and observation towers for viewing the shyer birds. The permanent collection includes many rare and exotic species, including the largest flock of flamingos in captivity. An attractive tropical house has also been built to simulate rain forest conditions and provide a comfortable living environment for a wide variety of brilliantly-plumaged water birds and hummingbirds. The centre provides a fascinating day out for anyone with an interest in birds and the natural environment. The visitor centre includes indoor displays, a permanent exhibition area and a 100-seater cinema, as well as a restaurant and gift shop. (Open daily, 9.30am to 5pm, all year round.)

Tudor Arms Lodge, Shepherd's Patch, Slimbridge
Tel: 01453 890306 Fax: 01453 890103

Situated within half-a-mile of the famous Wildfowl and Wetlands Centre at Slimbridge, the **Tudor Arms Lodge** offers the finest food, drink and accommodation. This impressive pub, restaurant and bed and breakfast establishment stands beside the Gloucester-Sharpness canal, within easy reach of junctions 13 and 14 on the M5. The oldest part of the inn was originally built in the early 1800s to serve the workforce constructing the canal. It remained a small beer and cider house until the late 1950s when it was upgraded and granted a full licence.

Today, the Tudor Arms is a popular stopping place for the many leisure craft travelling between Gloucester and the Severn estuary. Delicious meals are served in the 'Rorty Crankle' restaurant, a former barn and hayloft which has been tastefully converted into an elegant eating place. An excellent range of snacks is also available in the bar every lunchtime and evening. Proprietor Rita Rock and her staff also provide high standard overnight accommodation. The twelve spacious and comfortably appointed guest rooms are contained within a purpose built extension which was added in 1990. The nine twin and three family rooms are each equipped with an en-suite bathroom, remote control TV, direct-dial telephone, radio alarm, hair dryer, complimentary toiletries and tea/coffee making facilities.

FRAMPTON-ON-SEVERN

This delightful village lies just off the B4071, four miles north of Slimbridge. When approaching the village from the south, the distant Welsh mountains form a dramatic backdrop on the far side of the Severn. Frampton is renowned for having one of the largest village greens in England, the 22 acre **Rosamund Green**, which incorporates a cricket ground and three ponds. It was formed when the marshy ground outside the gates of Frampton Court was drained in the 18th century. For those who enjoy the time-honoured combination of village cricket and good beer, the Bell Inn is conveniently situated overlooking the green.

Frampton Court is an outstanding example of a Georgian country house. Now Grade I listed, it was built in Palladian style in the 1730s by architect John Strachan. Inside, there is a wonderful collection of antique porcelain, period furniture, and fine paintings, including those made famous in the best-selling book *Frampton Flora*, published in 1985.

Although the house is screened from the green by trees, it is still possible to catch a glimpse of the imposing Vanbrugh-inspired chimneys and the elegant Gothic-style orangery designed by William Halfpenny. The latter has recently been converted into holiday accommodation. The grounds are inhabited by strutting peacocks and contain an ornamental reflecting canal and a unique octagonal tower which was built in the 17th century as a dovecote. Frampton Court is the seat of the Clifford family and is open throughout the year by appointment only. (Telephone 01452 740267.)

The Clifford family's former home, **Frampton Manor**, stands on the opposite side of the green. Built between the 12th and 16th centuries, this fine part timber-framed manor house is thought to be the birthplace of Jane Clifford, better known as Henry II's mistress 'Fair Rosamund', who bore him two children and lived in a house surrounded by a maze at Woodstock. Legend has it that jealous Queen Eleanor found her way through the labyrinth to Rosamund's bower by following a thread of the King's cloak. The Queen then did away with her rival by forcing her to drink poison. (Rosamund was subsequently buried at Godstow nunnery.) Frampton Manor still has a lovely old walled garden and is open all year round to parties of ten or more by written appointment only.

Situated at the southwestern edge of the village, Frampton's charming 14th century **Church of St Mary** is reached via a footpath across a low meadow. The church stands beside the **Sharpness Canal** which was built to allow seagoing vessels to continue up the Severn valley as far as Gloucester. The sight of a large ship passing along the canal within a few yards of the church can be impressive. Look out also for the nearby canal keeper's house which was built in unusual mock Doric style.

WHITMINSTER

Set in the Severn Vale at the foot of the Cotswold Hills, **Whitminster House** stands beside the River Frome in a delightful position between Frampton-on-Severn and Whitminster village. This is an ideal base from which to explore the beautiful Gloucestershire countryside and discover the many castles, gardens and other country houses for which the county is renowned. The perfect country house weekend has historically been the preserve of a privileged few, with a recipe which calls for a fine country house, acres of England's green and pleasant countryside, spacious gardens, rolling lawns and a private stretch of river where guests can relax and enjoy the company of friends while engaged in a variety of entertainments and activities.

Whitminster House, Whitminster Tel/Fax: 01452 740204

All this and much more can be found at Whitminster House. Once owned by Henry V and dating from before the Norman Conquest, it consists of a fascinating blend of architecture spanning a millennium. The west wing affords generous and comfortable accommodation for up to ten guests self-catering or up to six for the fully-catered theme weekends; the Stables Cottage opposite accommodates up to four more. The estate's self-catering cottages offer a good range of sizes and prices to suit most people, sleeping from 2 to 10, or 18 to 24. One property, Walk Close, has been designed on a single level especially to suit accompanied disabled visitors. Whitminster House is also a particularly attractive setting for wedding receptions, with the church only a few steps away, a choice of lawns for the marquee, and facilities for the bride and her family to dress in the house.

ARLINGHAM

The nine-mile long circumference of the Arlingham peninsula forms part of the **Severn Way** Shepperdine-Tewkesbury long distance walk. Along this stretch, the trail passes close to **Wick Court**, a part 13th century moated manor house which was extended 300 years later. The 200 foot **Barrow Hill** commands magnificent views as far as the Severn bridges, the Forest of Dean, Gloucester and the Cotswolds.

A settlement since the Iron Age, Arlingham takes its name from the Saxon term for 'village by the running water'. During the early Middle Ages, the land on which the village stands belonged to the Berkeley hundreds, although it was subsequently acquired by the monks of St Augustine's Abbey in Bristol who believed it to be near the point where, in the 7th century, St Augustine crossed the Severn on his way to convert the Welsh tribes to Christianity. From here, there are fine views across the river to Newnham and Westbury-on-Severn.

Nearby **St Augustine's Farm** was built on the site of a monastic house in the 16th century, and indeed parts of the original building still can be seen today. St Augustine's is perhaps better known, however, as an open working farm which offers an interesting day out to visitors of all ages. Children can watch the cows being milked in a herringbone parlour, meet and help feed the animals, or follow an interesting farm trail. There is also a display of historic farm memorabilia, a children's playground, and a refreshment area. (Open daily, except non-Bank Holiday Mondays, 11am to 5pm between mid-March and end October.)

EPNEY

Following the river upstream, the village of Epney is perhaps better known on the Continent than it is in the UK. Each year, thousands of three year old baby eels, or elvers, are exported from here to the Netherlands and other parts of Europe to replenish the stocks in the canals. The ramparts of a 600 year old castle which once belonged to the De Valence family can still be seen in the historic hamlet of **Moreton Valence**, a mile-and-a-half inland from Epney. The largely 15th century village church has an impressive Norman doorway which incorporates a sculpture of the Archangel Michael thrusting a spear into a dragon's mouth.

NASTEND

Delightful farmhouse accommodation can be found to the northeast of junction 13 on the M5 near the hamlet of Nastend. **Nastend Farm** offers well presented bed and breakfast which is ideal for all the family. Jackie and Graham have a small dairy herd and guests are invited to watch the cows being milked, or help in the daily running of the farm. The three spacious and comfortable bedrooms all have good modern facilities, and there is also a large garden with swings and a swimming pool. The farm offers some attractive walks along the wooded farm trail and is rated 2 crowns by the English Tourist Board.

Nastend Farm, Nastend, Near Stonehouse Tel: 01453 822300

STONEHOUSE

Located just one-and-a-half miles from junction 13 on the M5, the renowned **Stonehouse Court Hotel** is an impressive establishment which offers exceptional food, service and accommodation. It provides a very convenient and luxurious place for an overnight stopover; however, a visit for just one night will not do justice to this wonderful 17th century Grade II listed hotel which is set within six acres of parkland overlooking Stroud Water. Stonehouse Court is somewhere to relax in true comfort and style. To wander around the beautifully kept gardens observing the abundance of rare shrubs and plants is genuinely therapeutic after a hectic journey, and there is also the opportunity for some excellent fishing for those so inclined.

On entering Stonehouse Court, guests are immediately struck by the style and warmth of the interior, with its mellow oak panelling, soft lighting and superb open stone fireplaces. The 37 guest bedrooms all have en-suite facilities and are furnished in a style more in keeping with a country house than a hotel. Each room is equipped with colour television, telephone and tea/coffee making facilities. The charming panelled dining rooms offer both table d'hôte and à la carte menus, complemented by an extensive and carefully selected wine list. Lunch is available from 10.50am and dinner from 5.50pm. As one might expect, standards are high; the service is excellent and the staff throughout the hotel are both efficient and friendly.

Stonehouse Court Hotel, Stonehouse Tel: 01453 825155

Also on the outskirts of Stonehouse is **Oldends Farm**, a historically Grade II listed farmhouse surrounded by orchards and open fields which offers delightful accommodation. Located only two miles from junction 13 on the M5, this 100 acre working farm keeps a small herd of suckler cows with their calves and a stud of Welsh ponies. The house is comfortably furnished, with the family and twin rooms both having TVs and en-suite facilities; a further single room has its own bathroom across the landing. A substantial breakfast is provided, and there are plenty of places nearby to eat at lunchtime and in the evening. The Spa Inn, situated just 100 yards from the farm gate, was once renowned for the purifying properties of its mineral waters.

Oldends Farm, Oldends Lane, Stonehouse Tel: 01453 822135

FROCESTER

Some of the loveliest villages on the eastern margin of the Vale of Berkeley lie in the country lanes to the south of Stonehouse. The chapel in the centre of Frocester was built in 1680 using materials taken from the private chapel of nearby Frocester Court. The present owners of this handsome country house will usually allow visitors to look around their 180 foot medieval tithe barn, one of the finest in the country.

LEONARD STANLEY

The **Grey Cottage** is a circa 1807 Cotswold stone house which is situated on the edge of Leonard Stanley, just one mile from the A419, three miles from Junction 13 on the M5, and four miles from Stroud.

The Grey Cottage, Bath Road, Leonard Stanley, Near Stonehouse
Tel/Fax: 01453 822515

Owned and personally run for over a decade by Andrew and Rosemary Reeves, the property offers superb country-style bed and breakfast accommodation. All the first floor bedrooms have private facilities and are individually decorated and finished with those small personal touches that make one's stay enjoyable and free from worry. Breakfasts are delicious and full of variety, and the dinners, if required, are also of a very high standard, with diners' preferences being discussed at the time of booking. The garden is absolutely beautiful and a tribute to Andrew and Rosemary's green fingers. When they purchased the property, the grounds had suffered years of neglect, and it has taken a great deal of hard work to restore the garden to its former glory. There is ample car parking in the enclosed driveway and although unlicensed, the Grey Cottage operates an honesty bar for those desiring a tipple.

The village of Leonard Stanley contains the remains of a largely intact

Saxon chapel and a 12th century priory. The chapel still contains an early clock and some fine medieval carvings, despite having been used as a barn for many centuries. Henry VIII and Anne Boleyn are reputed to have visited Leonard Stanley in 1535 when the village was at the height of its wool-trading prosperity.

KING'S STANLEY

Situated a mile to the east of its sister village, the larger community of King's Stanley has roots going back to Roman times. The parish church is Norman in origin, but was comprehensively remodelled by the Victorians in 1876. The village also boasts one of the earliest nonconformist places of worship in the country, a Baptist church constructed in 1640. Another architectural first, Stanley Mill, can be found on the outskirts of the village. Built as England's first fireproof industrial building, it continues to be used for the manufacture of cloth to this day.

SELSLEY

This attractive village stands beside the B4066 Stroud to Dursley road, a little further east. The village is associated with the Marling family, wealthy Stroud mill owners who were responsible for building the local church. This unusual building is modelled on a church spotted by Sir Samuel Marling on his travels around Europe and features some exceptional stained glass by Rossetti and William Morris. The nearby Selsley Herb and Goat Farm is a thriving enterprise where visitors can learn how to cultivate herbs. There are also a dozen or so goats and baby kids, which sometimes can be bottle fed by visitors. Goats' milk and soft cheese are available at the farm shop which is open daily between 1 April and end September.

STROUD

For centuries, the old market town of Stroud was acclaimed as the capital of the Cotswold woollen industry. Its geographical position on the River Frome at the point where five Cotswold valleys converge made it an ideal centre for cloth manufacturing in the 15th and 16th centuries. The surrounding hill farms provided a consistent supply of raw wool, while the fast-flowing Cotswold streams provided the water-power. By the 1820s, there were over 150 textile mills in the immediate locality and the town became famous for producing broadloom fabrics and 'Stroudwater scarlet', a thick, brightly-coloured cloth used for making military uniforms. Today, however, only six mills survive, including one specialising in green baize for snooker tables.

For a town with such a long and colourful history, Stroud makes a somewhat disappointing first impression. Centuries of unbroken economic renewal have left it without the quantity of fine old buildings one might expect. However, the centre does contain a number of interesting enclaves which are best explored on foot. Stroud's carefully-restored Tudor **Old Town Hall** dates from 1594 and is believed to be the oldest building in the town. It contains some fine stonework and a well, and stands in the heart a fascinating area known the Shambles, the old commercial market which still plays host to a busy weekly market.

Situated a short distance away in George Street, the Stroud Subscription Rooms have a splendid classical façade featuring a porte-cochére with Tuscan columns and a balustraded balcony above. The building also incorporates the George Room art gallery where regular exhibitions of work by locally and nationally renowned artists are held. For those interested in second-hand and antiquarian books, the excellent Inprint Bookshop in the High Street is a must. The imposing Medieval Hall, now a flourishing shop and restaurant, is situated nearby.

Ming Court, 17 Gloucester Street, Stroud
Tel: 01453 763758/753068

A very warm welcome is extended to customers old and new at **Ming Court**, a wonderful restaurant that serves authentic Peking and Szechuan cuisine at very affordable prices. Conveniently located in the very centre of Stroud, Ming Court offers visitors a warm traditional welcome and friendly efficient service. The restaurant is fully licensed and the menu extensive and varied. Dishes range from Deep fried crispy chilli beef and Roast duck in orange sauce to Scallops with ginger and spring onions and Prawns in tomato sauce. The fragrant crispy duck is absolutely delicious and is served with all the traditional accompaniments. A wide selection of wines is also available, as well as the usual beers and spirits. Perfect for functions or Christmas parties, Ming Court is open seven days a week, except Sunday lunchtimes, and also offers a comprehensive take-away service.

Some fine examples of early industrial mill architecture can be found on the edge of Stroud at Lodgemoor and Ebley. Similarly, **Rooksmoor Mill** on the Bath Road is a handsome 19th century woollen mill which has been converted into a flourishing business offering a wide selection of crafts and giftware. Stroud's highly regarded **Cowle Museum** in Lansdown is currently undergoing a major redevelopment and is due to open in a different location in 1999. Nearby Lansdown Hall features a display of local crafts and industrial artefacts. (Open Mondays to Saturdays, all year round; admission free.)

Cowle Museum, Stroud

Situated near the Paganhill Maypole on the western edge of Stroud is the **Paganhill Arch**, a Cotswold stone memorial erected to commemorate the 1833 Emancipation Act which ended slavery in the British colonies. The memorial once marked the entrance to Henry Wyatt's estate on Farmhill.

RANDWICK

Conveniently situated at Randwick to the northwest of Stroud, within easy driving distance of the M5, M4 and main trunk roads, **Court Farm** has many places of natural beauty and historic interest close at hand. Diana and John Taylor extend a warm welcome at this pretty 17th century beamed farmhouse which enjoys panoramic views of the beautiful Cotswold valleys. They offer accommodation in three comfortable guest rooms, with a full English breakfast and delicious evening meals, if required.

Court Farm, Randwick, Near Stroud Tel: 01453 764210

WOODCHESTER

The ancient settlement of Woodchester lies beside the A46 Bath road as it climbs into the Cotswolds to the south of Stroud. This is the location of one of the largest archeological sites of its kind in Britain, a Roman villa which covers some 26 acres. When the site was originally excavated in 1796, it was found to contain some impressive mosaics and other remains; however, the question then arose of how these could best be preserved. After a great deal of deliberation, the decision was made to re-bury the entire site, and so the only way to see the remains at first hand is to view one of the small sections that are re-exhumed and put on show from time to time.

AMBERLEY

Situated to the east of the A46 one-and-a-half miles south of Woodchester, Amberley has a surprising amount to offer the casual visitor. The village contains a privately owned 13th century castle, a church dating from 1837 which was once described by a former Bishop of Gloucester as 'the ugliest in Gloucestershire', the grave in the churchyard of PC Wren, the author of *Beau Geste*, and Rose Cottage where writer Mrs Craik worked on her Cotswold novel *John Halifax, Gentleman*.

Amberley is also the home of the **Chalk Pits Museum** (open 11am to 5pm on Wednesdays to Sundays between June and October), and the **Fine Arts Centre**, which offers courses in, and mounts regular exhibitions of, painting and photography. For those interesting in seeing the Cotswolds from the basket of a hot-air balloon, flights are offered from nearby Culver Hill.

MINCHINHAMPTON

A mile-and-a-half further east, the scattered Cotswold community of Minchinhampton stands on the ridge between the Golden and Nailsworth Valleys. The town's market charter is believed to date back to 1213, and at one time, the surrounding land was owned by the nuns of Caen. Following the Dissolution of the Monasteries, Henry VIII presented Minchinhampton Manor to the first Baron Windsor in return for the baron's existing family estate near Windsor, a forced exchange which netted the king a prime piece of property he'd apparently had his eye on for some time.

In 1651, the manor was acquired by Samuel Sheppard, whose descendant, Edward, built Gatcombe Park, the present country residence of the Princess Royal. Another member of the Sheppard family, Philip, was responsible for constructing the Market House in the centre of

Minchinhampton which was once an important wool trading hall. Now more commonly used as an auditorium, it is open to visitors by appointment only at weekends between 9am and 5.30pm.

Hunters Lodge, Dr Brown's Road, Minchinhampton, Near Stroud
Tel: 01453 883588 Fax: 01453 731449

Hunters Lodge is a beautifully decorated and furnished old Cotswold stone house which offers some of the finest bed and breakfast accommodation in the area. Situated 650 feet above Stroud in the charmingly named Dr Brown's Road, it adjoins 600 acres of National Trust land on Minchinhampton Common. Helpful hosts Margaret and Peter invite their guests to use the visitors' lounge, with its comfortable relaxed atmosphere, remote control colour TV and interesting selection of books, maps and magazines to browse through. On warmer days the delightful conservatory and large garden are also available. The three centrally heated guest bedrooms are individually decorated and equipped with en-suite or private bathrooms, washbasins and tea/coffee trays, with dressing gowns provided as a thoughtful extra.

Hunters Lodge is a superb base from which to explore the surrounding villages, whose many restaurants and country inns are ideal for eating out at lunchtime or in the evening. Menus of several eating places in the area are available on request. Peter, a Gloucestershire Green Badge Tourist Guide, is happy to help guests plan their visits to the many local places of interest, including those that are off the main tourist track.

Cotswold stone has long been quarried around Minchinhampton and at nearby **Ball's Green**, freestone mines extend underground for over a mile. The material used for facing the inside of the Houses of Parliament was quarried here in the 19th century. The steep-sided plateau to the south of Minchinhampton supports some of the last remaining common land in the Cotswolds. Now under the ownership of the National Trust, Minchinhampton and Rodborough Commons amount to almost 1000 acres of high woodland and open grassland which are rich in wild flora and fauna.

A number of important archeological sites can also be found here, including the remains of the Iron Age defences known as **Minchinhampton Bulwarks**, the Neolithic long barrow known as **Whitefield's Tump**, and the six-way crossroads known as **Tom Long's Post** which is named after the notorious highwayman was hanged close by. Whitefield's Tump achieved notoriety when the great Methodist preacher George Whitefield made a famous public address from its summit in 1743.

NAILSWORTH

This small residential and commercial town, on the A46 to the southwest of Minchinhampton, like many of its neighbours was once a centre of the wool trade. Its centre contains some fine Jacobean and Georgian merchants' houses, and an unusual 17th century building on Cossack Square known as Stokescroft. Also referred to locally as 'the barracks', graffiti uncovered during restoration work in 1972 suggests that local troops were billeted here in 1812 and 1815. It was also used to house Russian prisoners during the Crimean War, an episode which is commemorated in the unusual name of the square.

Several of Nailsworth's original mills have been modernised and continue in a manufacturing role. Others have been given a new life, for example Egypt Mill, a former grain and logging mill with two working water wheels, has been converted to a popular family pub. **Ruskin Mill** is a 19th century former woollen mill which has been rejuvenated as a thriving craft centre. Inspired by the principles of William Morris, John Ruskin and Rudolph Steiner, this vibrant place incorporates an exhibition gallery, a vegetarian café, and a series of traditional craft workshops covering such skills as cobbling, woodworking and stained glass. (Open Tuesdays to Saturdays 11am to 4pm, and Sundays and Bank Holiday Mondays 3pm to 6pm, all year round.)

Aaron Farm, Nympsfield Road, Nailsworth
Tel: 01453 833598

Standing in an elevated position on the western edge of Nailsworth, **Aaron Farm** is an impressive bed and breakfast establishment which enjoys spectacular views over the surrounding countryside. The home of resident proprietor June Mulligan, this handsome former farmhouse has been refurbished to provide exceptionally spacious accommodation of a very high standard. All the guest rooms are en-suite with tea/coffee making facilities, colour television and full central heating; non-smokers are preferred.

As well as commanding extensive views of the local landscape, Aaron Farm is situated within easy reach of the many local amenities and places of interest.

The **Upper House** is a delightful bed and breakfast establishment which is situated to the west of Nailsworth town centre. Owned and personally run since 1991 by Angela and Myles Robinson, this spacious detached house provides a warm welcome and charming hospitality. Guests can choose between a double, twin or family room, each complete with en-suite facilities, colour TV and a beautiful view over the surrounding countryside. There is also a light and airy guest sitting room, and a dining room with doors leading onto the patio area which is attractively decorated in traditional country style.

Situated between Bath and Cheltenham, the Upper House has ample parking and is an ideal base for touring the region. There are also plenty of restaurants and country inns in the surrounding villages to provide guests with delicious lunches and evening meals.

The Upper House, Spring Hill, Nailsworth
Tel: 01453 836606

Set in the beautiful Avening Valley on the southeastern side of Nailsworth, the **Waterside Garden Centre** offers a vast range of plants, from unusual varieties to everyday favourites. As well as specialising in plants

Waterside Garden Centre, Avening Road, Nailsworth
Tel: 01453 833899 Fax: 01453 834824

and all the associated sundries, the Waterside Centre offers a garden design service, a comprehensive selection of furniture for conservatories and outdoor use, a range of garden buildings from greenhouses to live-in log cabins, and a wide choice of gifts, books and food items. Customers can also enjoy delicious home-made food overlooking the lake in the informal atmosphere of Tubby's Restaurant.

AVENING

The ancient village of Avening lies two-and-a-half miles to the southeast of Nailsworth along the B4014 Tetbury road. The village church dates from just four years after the Norman Conquest. Inside, there is a memorial to the Hon Henry Bridge, the infamous 17th century highwayman who in his youth is reported to have carried out 'deeds of lawlessness and robbery almost unsurpassed'. The remarkable **Avening Long Stone** can be seen in Hampton Fields, just off the B4014 to the northeast of the village. Measuring eight feet in height and pierced with holes, this mysterious prehistoric standing stone has been known to move on Midsummer's Eve, at least if one is to believe the local legend.

Each year on the Sunday nearest 14 September, Avening celebrates 'Pig Face Sunday', an unusual festival originating in the days when wild boar roamed freely in the Cotswolds. Boar could cause a great deal of damage to crops and were known to attack domestic animals and even humans. Indeed, one rogue animal is said to have caused such havoc that when it was finally caught, it was 'hung from a sturdy oak before being roasted and eaten', a custom of which continues in an updated form to this day.

The **Bell Inn** is a typical country pub which is situated in Avening's leafy main street. Recent new owners Kevin and Janet are a very welcoming and hospitable couple who have already established an excellent rapport with both locals and visitors alike. They serve a good selection of traditional ales and a wide choice of unpretentious meals and snacks of good quality and value. They also offer comfortable bed and breakfast accommodation in two well appointed guest bedrooms. Those looking for an honest local pub without any chrome or pretentious trimmings will do well to call in at the Bell. Children are welcome, although no pets please.

The Bell Inn, 29 High Street, Avening, Near Nailsworth
Tel: 01453 836422

Chavenage House is situated to the west of the B4014, midway between Avening and Tetbury. This beautiful Elizabethan mansion is built of mellow grey Cotswold stone in the characteristic 'E' shape of the period.

The elegant front aspect has remained virtually unchanged since Edward Stephens added the porch and wings to the former manor house in 1576. The Stephens family were exceedingly wealthy at the time, although over the years their fortune dwindled away and for a while, the estate had to be heavily mortgaged. Chavenage nevertheless remained in the family, and the present owners, the Lowsley-Williams, can trace their lineage back to the original Stephens in a line broken only by marriage.

The superb interior is furnished with rare 17th century tapestries, period furniture, fine paintings and relics of the Cromwellian era. Cromwell is known to have stayed at Chavenage and two of the loveliest tapestry rooms were set aside to accommodate him. The main hall is spanned by a wide screen, the upper part of which forms a delightful minstrels' gallery, and there is also a charming family chapel which is separated from the house by a narrow passage. The chapel tower was built as a folly in the early 1700s and the rest of the building, which has some amusing gargoyles incorporated into the masonry, was added some 100 years later. The infamous Legend of Chavenage dates from the English Civil War when the owner of the estate died after being cursed by his daughter and was taken away in a coach driven by a headless horseman. (Open Thursdays, Sundays and Bank Holiday Mondays, 2pm to 5pm between May and September.)

Chavenage House

TETBURY

The delightful Elizabethan market town of Tetbury stands at the junction of the A433, A4135 and B4014, two miles south of Chavenage. Another important centre of the once prosperous Cotswold wool trade, at one time fleeces were weighed and sold amongst the stone pillars of the 17th century Market House in the heart of the town. Today, this striking colonnaded building hosts a popular antiques market and the immediate area is filled with market stalls offering a wide range of produce from fresh fruit and vegetables to handmade local crafts.

One of the most delightful attractions in Tetbury is the **Tetbury Gallery and Tea Room** which is situated within a few yards of the Market House in the town centre. The gallery features a selection of paintings and other fine art which is carefully chosen by proprietors Jane Maile and Helen Joyner. Open seven days a week, the tea room has a quintessentially

English atmosphere, with linen tablecloths and pure white china, and is a perfect place to enjoy a delicious morning coffee, light lunch or traditional clotted cream tea. The food is exceptional and features a mouthwatering selection of home-made soups, salads, hot savouries, scones and cakes. In fine weather, customers can sit in the delightful walled courtyard to the rear.

Tetbury Gallery and Tea Room, 18 Market Place, Tetbury
Tel: 01666 503412

Chipping Lane connects the Market House to **The Chipping**, a word meaning 'market' or 'trading centre' in Old English, via the famous Chipping Steps. This ancient stairway descends past a collection of charming stepped houses which are among the most handsome in Tetbury. The parish **Church of St Mary** was restored in 1781 at the height of town's wool-trading prosperity. Considered an 18th century period piece, the interior features pews with unusually high backs and huge windows made from recovered medieval glass. The ceiling appears to be supported on slender timber columns; however, these conceal strong iron uprights, an example of a cunning and innovative building system of its day.

The **Close Hotel and Restaurant** is a superb establishment which is part of Richard Branson's Virgin Group. Set around a beautiful courtyard garden in the heart of Tetbury, this impressive town house was originally constructed in 1585 for John Seede, a yeoman farmer who rose to become a prosperous wool-merchant. Since then, it has undergone a number of improvements, perhaps the most significant being the addition of fine Adam ceilings in the mid-1800s which are still in place today. The building has been completely restored and refurbished by its present owners. The public rooms retain the feel of a luxurious yet intimate private home, and the guest bedrooms are beautifully-appointed and fitted with en suite bathrooms, colour televisions and a range of sumptuous extras. Each has an individual name, such as 'Tower', 'Doves', 'Estcourt' and 'Gallery', and several have the added luxury of a four-poster bed. The award winning restaurant is renowned for its cuisine, fine wines and charming, discreet service; an elegant room enhanced by fine glass, porcelain, silverware and linen, it looks out across the terrace to the garden beyond.

Close Hotel and Restaurant, Long Street, Tetbury
Tel: 01666 502272 Fax: 01666 504401

Standing adjacent to the tourist information office in Long Street, Tetbury's Old Court House and police station now house the **Police Bygones Museum**, an interesting collection of historic artefacts, uniforms and memorabilia from the archives of the Gloucestershire Constabulary. (Open Monday to Saturday, 10am to 4.15pm between Easter and end October; admission free.)

The **Crown Inn** in Gumstool Hill, Tetbury provides an excellent base for touring the attractive countryside of the southern Cotswolds. Situated in the heart of the town, this handsome 17th century former coaching inn offers a wide selection of ales, fine wines, good food and accommodation. Proprietors Jo and Ian Wainwright have created a wonderful atmosphere which is welcoming to visitors and locals alike. Even the resident ghost, whose appearance has been personally witnessed by Ian, is known to be friendly. A full range of drinks is available at the bar, and the no smoking conservatory-restaurant offers an extensive menu at refreshingly reasonable prices. Comfortable accommodation is also available in four well appointed guest bedrooms.

Crown Inn, Gumstool Hill, Tetbury Tel: 01666 502469

Tetbury's gruelling annual **Woolsack Race** starts and finishes outside the Crown Inn. Race competitors have to run up and down nearby Gumstool Hill, one of the steepest in Gloucestershire. (The name 'Gumstool' is derived from the ducking stools which were used to inflict a damp and cruel torture on those accused of antisocial crimes or witchcraft.)

Royal Oak Inn, Tetbury Tel: 01666 502570

Situated on the old Cirencester road out of Tetbury, the **Royal Oak Inn** is a charming old pub which offers a warm welcome and excellent food and drink. A wide selection of home-cooked dishes can be ordered at the bar and enjoyed in a relaxed atmosphere which is full of character and charm. The prices are surprisingly reasonable, and there is an impressive choice of traditional ales and other drinks to accompany the meal. For those with an interest in the supernatural, hosts Tony and Janet Peace have recently reopened a room which was sealed in the 1950s because of unwelcome paranormal activity. At the time of writing, they were still waiting to see what happens...

BEVERSTONE

The attractive community of Beverstone lies two miles west of Tetbury on the A4135 Dursley road. This unusual model village was built by Victorian estate owner Robert Stayner Holford, a noted connoisseur of the Renaissance period, in conjunction with architect Lewis Vulliamy. The layout was designed to combine rural practicality with improved standards of accommodation. The golden Cotswold limestone terraces, cottages and model farms can be seen from the main road running through the village. Beverstone's medieval parish church has a tower containing a marvellous, if somewhat damaged, sculpture of the Resurrection which is thought to date from before the Norman Conquest. At this time, Beverstone had an important castle which was occupied by Earl Godwin, the father of King Harold. The remains of this rare Saxon fortification can be seen down a side road.

Beverstone's patron, RS Holford, lived at **Westonbirt House**, two miles to the south, an imposing country mansion which is now a celebrated private girls' school. Its magnificent 22 acre grounds are a product of the once fashionable practice of emparking, the process by which all buildings within sight of the main house, except in this case the church, were removed and rebuilt a discreet distance away in order to give uninterrupted views over the estate. **Westonbirt Gardens** are open to the public on a number of days each year under the National Gardens Scheme.

The internationally renowned **Westonbirt Arboretum** is situated adjacent to Westonbirt Gardens off the A433 Tetbury to Chipping Sodbury road. Founded in 1829 and now incorporated into a 600 acre Forestry Commission estate, this unique attraction began as another of Robert Stayner Holford's imaginative ventures. An amateur enthusiast with a great love of trees, Holford began planting for his own pleasure. In the course of time, he passed on his passion to his son, Sir George Holford, who continued to work with even greater zeal until 1926 when he died and was succeeded by his nephew, the fourth Earl of Morley. In 1956, the arboretum was acquired by Forest Enterprise who opened it to the general public for the first time.

The grounds now contain some 18,000 trees and shrubs from all over the globe, one of the largest and most important collections in the world. Some plants are very rarely found in cultivation, others are extinct in the wild, their only refuge being collections such as this. Because Westonbirt is primarily a research and conservation establishment there is always something going on. The spring flowering shrubs in April and May, and the autumn foliage colours in October are perhaps the most spectacular attractions, but the arboretum is beautiful at all times of the year.

Visitors can choose to join a guided walk or wander freely throughout the grounds. Selected sections of the seventeen miles of paths and glades have been formed into waymarked walks, and a useful trail guide can be purchased at the visitor centre. This also contains an interesting exhibition area, a video presentation and a gift shop. There is a pleasant café nearby, and picnic tables are provided adjacent to the car park. (Open daily, 10am to 5pm, all year round.)

KNOCKDOWN

Some of the finest farmhouse accommodation in the area can be found at **Avenue Farm**, a traditional working farm which lies on the Wiltshire-Gloucestershire border in the charmingly named hamlet of Knockdown. It is easy to find off the A433 Tetbury to Chipping Sodbury road, half-a-mile southwest of Westonbirt Arboretum and just a few minutes' drive from junction 18 on the M4. The delightful family home of Sonja and James King, the farmhouse is over three centuries old. In recent years it has been fully refurbished and modernised, and now offers three attractive guest bedrooms, all with en-suite showers and a number of thoughtful extras. Each room is very comfortable and well-appointed, and has a special character all of its own.

Avenue Farm, Knockdown, Near Tetbury Tel: 01454 238207
Fax: 01666 840303

Indeed, the atmosphere throughout the whole of Avenue Farm is friendly and full of genuine Cotswold character. Sonja and James are charming hosts who provide the warmest of welcomes and a superb full English breakfast. Sonja makes her own bread and marmalade, and serves fresh eggs from her son-in-law's flock of free range hens which often can be seen around the farmyard. With part of its land adjoining the beautiful Westonbirt Arboretum, Avenue Farm is an ideal base for visiting the many fine attractions of the southern Cotswolds, including the centres of Bath, Cirencester and Stroud.

DIDMARTON

This attractive village lies a couple of miles along the A433 to the southwest of Knockdown. This is the location of the now disused **Church of St Lawrence**, a charming medieval building standing beside a towering Wellingtonia which still remains open to visitors. Unlike most of its contemporaries which were remodelled by the Victorians, it has not been altered since the 18th century. Its original three storey pulpit and set of antique box pews painted in Georgian green can still be seen, and to the rear, there is a surprising row of hat pegs set sixteen feet above the floor, evidence that the church was either frequented by a congregation of giants, or once had an upper gallery.

Those looking for exceptional bed and breakfast accommodation in this delightful part of the Cotswolds should make a point of finding **The Folly**. Set in a secluded backwater off the A433, this handsome 17th century country residence has the relaxed atmosphere of a traditional family home, with old timber beams, log fires and an inglenook fireplace. Proprietors Daphne and Myles Marchington provide a warm welcome and an excellent Cotswold breakfast; they also offer delicious evening meals by arrangement. The house is adorned with clematis and roses and is set in a beautiful garden with its own tennis court. Unsuitable for smokers.

The Folly, Didmarton, Near Tetbury Tel: 01454 238618

Didmarton also contains a crumbling 17th century manor house which is set back from the church behind the Wellingtonia. On the other side of the road, a curious semicircle of stones marks the site of **St Lawrence's Well**. According to local legend, St Lawrence himself visited the spot in the 6th century, and after blessing the well, he promised the inhabitants it would never run dry. **Kingsmead House** in the centre of Didmarton stands out from its neighbours owing to its unusual octagonal gazebo. This was strategically built beside the highway to allow its owner to get an early glimpse of the coaches arriving from Bath. The garden also contains an interesting Gothic hermit's house made of yew wood.

LEIGHTERTON

A minor country road to the north of Didmarton leads to the secluded village of Leighterton, a community containing some pretty stone cottages, a pleasant looking inn, and a churchyard filled with characteristic dark leafed yew trees. The church tower is unusual in that it has a timber belfry and an oak spire.

ALDERLEY

The country lanes to the west of Leighterton descend into a wooded vale near the village of Alderley, another pleasant community with a castellated church and a handsome Elizabethan manor house which has been converted into a school. The gardens of **Alderley Grange** at Brackenbury are noted for their fine aromatic plants, herbs and old fashioned roses, and are open from time to time under the National Gardens Scheme. Also of interest is the nearby **Alderley Trout Farm**.

WORTLEY

Some impressive Roman remains can be seen a mile to the north of Alderley in the village of Wortley. Fragments of a luxurious Roman villa were discovered here in 1981 when some local people digging a hole for a fence post unearthed a section of mosaic floor. Further excavation revealed a six-roomed bath house complex built in two phases, a paved courtyard dating from the 3rd century, and some massive stone drain-blocks. A small museum on the site displays a selection of the many hundreds of items found here during the excavations. (Open 2pm to 5pm between mid-June and end September.)

WOTTON-UNDER-EDGE

This small country town straddles the ridge of the Cotswold escarpment, a mile to the north of Wortley. For centuries, this historic community was involved in the wool and silk trade, and at one time it contained as many as thirteen textile mills. Several handsome 17th and 18th century town houses remain, built in a mixture of styles from traditional Cotswold stone to the half-timbered brick more characteristic of the Severn Vale. The top floors of many once served as family weaving rooms.

Other noteworthy buildings in Wotton include the **Perry** and **Dawes Almshouses**, which were built in 1632 around a hidden cobbled quadrangle in Church Street, and **Tolsey House**, an early brick structure on the corner of Market Street which once functioned as a toll house for the market. The town also has a 14th century school and a fine 13th to 15th century **Church** dedicated to St Mary the Virgin which was substantially refurbished on the wealth of the wool and cloth trade. The room above the porch once contained a collection of rare books which are now housed at Christ Church, Oxford. The church also has an interesting organ which was originally installed at St Martin-in-the-Fields in London and is said to have been played by Handel.

A house in Orchard Street was once the family home of Isaac Pitman, a local schoolmaster who devised the world-renowned system of shorthand which still bears his name.

One of the most interesting industrial buildings in the town is an imposing gabled woollen mill dating from around 1800 which has a distinctive clock tower and large mill pond. The site still operates as a textile factory, and although the old buildings are now disused, they can be visited by appointment. Inside, there are a number of interesting industrial relics, including a wool stove and a circular kiln which was used to dry washed wool.

For those with a special interest in the history of the locality, Wotton-under-Edge Historical Society's Library and Museum is situated adjacent to the main library in Ludgate Hill. The library contains a fascinating collection of books, documents, maps, photographs and historic ephemera, and is open on Saturdays from 10am to 12 noon and on summer Tuesdays from 2.30pm to 4.30pm; admission free.

Overlooking the Coombe Valley and lying only one mile from the centre of Wotton-under-Edge, **Coombe Lodge** is a family run Georgian country house which extends a warm welcome to all its guests. The three spacious and centrally heated guest bedrooms all have washbasins, TVs and beverage making facilities, and one has the added luxury of a four-poster bed. Guests can experience the welcome change of a delicious vegetarian breakfast served in the elegant Victorian dining room. The sitting room provides an extensive range of local guides and maps, and there is also a relaxing sauna which provides the perfect way to round off a satisfying day.

Coombe Lodge, Wotton-under-Edge Tel: 01453 845057
Fax: 01453 521233

OZLEWORTH

A mile-and-a-half to the east of Wotton-under-Edge, the secluded hamlet of Ozleworth is worth visiting for its unusual circular churchyard, one of only two in England. The **Church**, which has a rare six-sided Norman tower rising from its centre, is thought to stand on a site which has been a holy place since pagan times.

Ozleworth is also the location of the National Trust-owned **Newark Park**, an impressive former hunting lodge built near a precipice by the Poyntz family in Elizabethan times. Major alterations carried out by James Wyatt in 1790 created a four-square castellated country house. Today, the house and garden are undergoing further renovation coordinated by the present tenant, who is also responsible for showing visitors round. (Open by appointment on Mondays only, 11am to 6pm between June and September, plus group visits at other times by special arrangement.)

The countryside around Ozleworth offers some fine walks, including one which takes in the Midger Wood Nature Reserve on its way up to **Nan Tow's Tump**, a huge round barrow which, at some 100 feet in diameter, is one of the largest and most mysterious Bronze Age burial mounds in the west of England. The tomb at its centre is thought to contain the remains of Nan Tow, a local witch who is alleged to have been buried in an upright position.

NORTH NIBLEY

This village is the birthplace of the early biblical translator, William Tyndale. Born here around 1494, he is reputed to be the first scholar to translate the New Testament into English and it is upon his work that the authorised version of the Bible was based. Instead of using the approved Latin texts, Tyndale chose to use original Greek and Hebrew sources, a choice which eventually led to him being accused of heresy. In 1536, he was arrested and taken to Vilvorde near Brussels where he was convicted and burned at the stake.

Some 330 years later, the impressive **Tyndale Monument** was erected on the ridge above North Nibley to commemorate the life and work of this pioneering scholar. From its position on top of the 700 foot Cotswold escarpment, the 111 foot structure can be seen from miles around, making it one of the most prominent landmarks on the Cotswold Way. North Nibley is also renowned as the site of the last 'private' battle in England which took place in 1471 between the rival barons William Lord Berkeley and the Viscount De Lisle.

STINCHCOMBE

This charming village lies on the western side of the B4060, a couple of miles to the north of North Nibley. Sheltered to the east by Stinchcombe Hill, this picturesque community contains a number of noteworthy buildings, including the 17th century **Melksham House**, seat of the Tyndale family for over 300 years, and the 18th century **Piers Court**, home of author Evelyn Waugh.

Stancombe Park, on the southern side of Stinchcombe, is a fine country residence which was built in 1880 on the site of a Roman villa. The villa's superb mosaic floor was painstakingly removed and is now on display in Gloucester museum. The grounds of the house are open to the public for a limited number of days each year under the National Gardens Scheme.

CAM

The ancient village of Cam lies on the eastern side of the A4135, two miles east of Stinchcombe. Despite its modern urban appearance the settlement dates from the 11th century when its manor, then known as Camma, formed part of the huge Berkeley estate. The village has been a cloth-making centre for centuries and today, Cam Mill carries on the tradition which began on the site in 1522. Cam's Hopton Manor School was founded in 1730 and is thought to be one of the oldest primary schools in the country.

The small, uniformly-shaped hill on the edge of the village is known as

Cam Long Down. This strange, isolated peak is steeped in local mythology. It is said that the Devil, thinking the landscape too much God's country, decided to cart away the Cotswolds to dam the Severn. After loading up his first barrow and setting out towards the river, he met a cobbler laden with shoes. 'How far is it to the river?' asked Satan. The cobbler showed him one of the shoes he was taking home to mend and replied, 'Do you see this sole? Well, I've worn it out walking from the Severn.' At this point, the Devil abandoned his task and tipped out his barrow, leaving behind the unusual formation that can be seen today.

Cam Long Down is also one of several places rumoured to be the site of King Arthur's final battle. According to some accounts, he crossed the River Severn and confronted his enemies at a place known as 'Camlann'. Whether or not either legend is true, a strange mystical atmosphere persists here to this day.

DURSLEY

On the A4135 to the south of Cam, Dursley is a small town with something of an industrial feel. Its impressive 18th century Market House has an interesting bell turret on the roof and overhanging upper storeys which are supported on pillars. Inside, there is a statue of Queen Anne and the distinctive coat of arms of the Estcourt family. Dursley also possesses a fine parish church which was constructed in the 14th and 15th centuries. William Shakespeare is rumoured to have spent some months laying low in the town after having been spotted poaching Thomas Lacy's deer at Charlecote. One legacy of his stay is a reference in *Henry IV* to a bailiff from Dursley.

ULEY

The delightful old cloth-making village of Uley is spread along the B4066 Stroud road, two-and-a-half miles to the east of Dursley. Its tranquil atmosphere conceals the fact that the village was once a hive of commercial activity. As long ago as 1608, it was recorded that three local cloth-merchants earned a living from marketing the products of 29 local weavers, most of whom produced high quality broadcloth.

The **Kings Head** at Uley is a handsome old Cotswold inn with a long and interesting past. Full of genuine character, this attractive establishment is popular with visitors and local residents alike. Improvements and general updating of the interior and facilities have created a really terrific atmosphere. Hosts Christine and Graham provide a very warm welcome, fine ales and delicious food, with children being well catered for. They also have two comfortable guest rooms available for those wishing to extend their stay. A genuine piece of old England, the Kings Head is well worth a visit.

Kings Head, 14 The Street, Uley, Near Dursley Tel: 01453 860282

Set in formal terraced gardens on the edge of Uley, **Owlpen Manor** is a handsome Tudor country house which, along with its church and outbuildings, forms a superb Cotswold manorial group. The house contains some unique 17th century wall hangings, a rare beadwork collection and some fine pieces of Cotswold Arts and Crafts furniture. There is also a pleasant restaurant in the medieval tithe barn serving lunches and afternoon teas. (Open Tuesdays to Sundays, 2pm to 5pm between April and October.)

The village of Uley lies in the shadow of **Uley Bury**, a massive Iron Age hill fort whose outer perimeter is marked by a series of banked ditches. The fort's 32 acre interior is mostly given over to the cultivation of arable crops and remains largely unexcavated. A number of artefacts have been uncovered here in recent years which show evidence that the fort was inhabited by a prosperous community of warrior farmers during the 1st century BC. Items discovered include bronze, glass and shale jewellery, iron ingots (a form of currency) and gold coins which have been attributed to the Dobunni tribe within whose lands Uley Bury is situated.

Another impressive prehistoric site, **Uley Long Barrow**, lies a mile along the Cotswold ridge to the north. Known locally as **Hetty Pegler's Tump**, this 180 foot long Neolithic burial site takes its name from Hester Pegler, a member of a 17th century land-owning family who lived nearby. Those brave enough to creep along the barrow's low entrance passage will discover four burial chambers where as many as 38 skeletons were discovered in the 19th century. Torchlight reveals the walls and ceilings to be constructed of huge stone slabs infilled with dry-stone material. Keys to Hetty Pegler's Tump can be obtained from Crawley Hill Farm, half-a-mile to the south on the B4066.

Coaley Peak, a mile-and-a-half further north, is the site of another spectacular Neolithic chambered tomb, **Nympsfield Long Barrow**. The climb to the summit is rewarded with magnificent views over the surrounding landscape.

Owlpen Manor

NYMPSFIELD

This is a pretty village with a renowned garden. For those interested in gliding, trial lessons and five day holiday courses are offered by the locally based Bristol and Gloucestershire Gliding Club (telephone 01453 860342).

Woodchester Park Mansion, whose entrance is situated near the Coaley Peak picnic area, is an uncompleted Gothic country house which was designed by Benjamin Bucknall. This unfinished masterpiece is currently finding a new life as a centre for training stonemasons and building conservationists in traditional methods of construction. The house is open to the public on the first complete weekend of every month, plus Bank Holiday weekends, 11am to 4pm between Easter and end October. (House unsuitable for children under 12 and dogs.) The grounds have recently been acquired by the National Trust and are open daily, 9am to 8pm (5pm in winter), all year round.

CHAPTER FOUR
Vale of Gloucester

Tewkesbury Abbey

Gloucester Cathedral

4
Vale of Gloucester

BROADWAY

Situated on the northern margin of the Cotswolds just before they fall away into the Vale of Evesham, Broadway is an exceptionally attractive settlement which has a well-deserved reputation for being the 'show village of England'. Many of the honey-coloured Cotswold stone buildings which line the unusually long and wide main street date back to Tudor and Jacobean times. In recent years, some have been converted into interesting antique shops and retail outlets designed to cater for passing visitors. The broad village green is overlooked by **St Michael's Parish Church** and the Broadway Hotel, and a short distance away, the former 16th century private residence which is now the Lygon Arms Hotel stands beside the famous furniture workshops belonging to Gordon Russell Ltd.

One of Broadway's attractions which definitely should not be missed is **Tisanes Tea Shop**, a charming shop which stocks one of the widest selections of teapots available anywhere in the UK. Teapots in every possible shape and form and offered for sale, from old petrol pumps, chests of drawers and toby jugs, to paint tins, cars, cottages and animals - almost anything that can be imagined! Proprietors Barrie and Jill are friendly people who are ready to help in any way they can. As well as teapots, they also provide fine teas and freshly ground coffees from all over the world. It's worth paying a visit just for the aroma! The tea shop itself looks out onto a small but very attractive patio garden where customers can sit and sample some of the exotic varieties for themselves. The menu also features freshly cut sandwiches, delicious cream teas, cakes and gateaux, all served in a most relaxed and congenial atmosphere.

Tisanes Tea Shop, Cotswold House, The Green, Broadway
Tel: 01386 852112

Lying just a short walk from the centre of Broadway, **Brook House**, on the A44 Evesham Road, is a Victorian villa which offers first-rate bed and breakfast accommodation. Resident proprietors Marianne and Owen Thomas are friendly hosts who have been in business for fourteen years.

Brook House, Station Road, Broadway Tel: 01386 852313

They offer good value for money in an area where, due to its popularity, prices tend to be higher than average. The bedrooms are centrally heated and have washbasins, televisions and tea/coffee making equipment; two also have en-suite facilities. A full English breakfast is provided, and children and pets are most welcome. There are also plenty of good places to eat in the immediate area.

A mile-and-a-half to the southeast of Broadway, Fish Hill rises to over 1000 feet and is topped by a highly conspicuous folly, the **Broadway Tower**, which was built in 1800 by the Earl of Coventry simply so that he could admire it from his home at Worcester nearly twenty miles away. The tower, with its spectacular views, once served as a retreat to William Morris, and so the Morris Room and the exhibitions on local history in this superb building are a must. (Open daily, 10am to 6pm between 1 April and 31 October.) A further exhibition, on Cotswold life during World War II, is housed in nearby Tower Barn.

Broadway Tower Country Park, Broadway Tel: 01386 852390

These outstanding buildings stand at the centre of a network of footpaths and nature trails which crisscross the scenic **Broadway Tower Country**

Park, a place offering a countryside experience with a difference. Set high in the Cotswolds, the park specialises in the breeding of red deer. Families will certainly find there is something here for everyone. Additional facilities include an adventure playground, giant chess and draughts, free use of barbecues and scenic walks. The Rookery Barn Restaurant on site is fully licensed, and game and venison are available in season or by pre-booking. Open daily throughout the year, the park offers a highly enjoyable experience and is well worth a visit.

A couple of miles further south, the National Trust-owned **Snowshill Manor** is an elegant small manor house dating from Tudor times which once belonged to Catherine Parr, the sixth wife of Henry VIII. The building has an attractive 17th century Cotswold stone façade and contains 21 rooms, most of which are open to the public. The rooms contain a fascinating collection of historic artefacts assembled over several decades by the last private owner, Charles Paget Wade.

Articles on display include clocks, toys, bicycles, sedan chairs, oriental furniture and nautical items such as compasses, telescopes and model ships. There are also a number of exhibits relating to Wade's special interest in the occult. Towards the end of his life, the collection became so large that Paget was forced to live in one of the outbuildings. (Snowshill Manor is open daily, except Tuesdays, 1pm to 6pm between April and end-October.)

CHILDSWICKHAM

Mount Pleasant Farm and Holiday Cottages, Hinton Road, Childswickham, Near Broadway Tel: 01386 853424

Lying three miles northwest of Broadway near the Worcestershire village of Childswickham, **Mount Pleasant Farm** is a 500 acre family run mixed farm with horses and other animals which offers delightful holiday accommodation. Bed and breakfast is provided at the farmhouse, which has been awarded 2 crowns and is highly commended by the English Tourist Board. The one single, one twin and two double rooms all have television, central heating, tea/coffee making facilities and magnificent views over the surrounding countryside. In the morning, a hearty farmhouse breakfast awaits! Mount Pleasant Farm also has a number of holiday cottages available which have been tastefully converted from lovely old barns to provide a high standard of accommodation. The farm is ideally situated for touring the Cotswolds, and Stratford-upon-Avon is only fifteen miles away. For further details contact Mrs Helen Perry.

BUCKLAND

A short drive to the southwest of Broadway leads to the village which is believed to contain the oldest rectory in England. Buckland is a peaceful and picturesque settlement which is situated under the crest of Burhill, just to the east of the B4632 Cheltenham road. The rectory dates from the Middle Ages and incorporates a 14th century great hall which has unusual hammerbeams carved with angels. One of the rectory windows dates from the 15th century and has a design attributed to the Malvern Priory school of glass making. John Wesley is said to have preached at the rectory which is open to visitors between 11am and 4pm on Mondays only during May, June, July and September; admission free.

There is also a fine Perpendicular church in Buckland with a 15th century east window which was restored in the 19th century on the instructions of William Morris, the Pre-Raphaelite designer and founder of the Arts and Crafts Movement. This lovely little building is surrounded by an interesting churchyard which contains an unusual table tomb and the graves of several locally-renowned luminaries.

Those looking for outstanding accommodation in this attractive part of the country should make a point of finding **Leasow House** at Laverton Meadows, a mile to the southwest of Buckland. As guests walk through the gate and up the path, they can immediately sense the atmosphere of this charming old country house. The setting is peaceful and the delightful 17th century house affords panoramic views of the Cotswold escarpment. Leasow House is personally run by Barbara and Gordon Meekings, charming hosts who have successfully created a pleasant informal atmosphere. Considerable thought has gone into furnishing the interior, which blends perfectly with the character of the house. All guest rooms have en-suite bathrooms or showers, TVs and drinks facilities, and a number of outbuildings have been tastefully converted to provide additional ground floor accommodation for disabled guests. English Tourist Board 2 crowns highly commended, RAC highly acclaimed and AA selected, Leasow House provides a superb base for touring the Cotswolds and the Vale of Evesham.

Leasow House, Laverton Meadows, Near Broadway
Tel: 01386 584526 Fax: 01386 584596

TEMPLE GUITING

The country lanes to the south of Snowshill lead across the B4077 at Ford to Temple Guiting, an exceptionally attractive north Cotswolds hamlet on the banks of the Upper Windrush which has a fine church and a handsome Georgian mansion. In the 12th century, the Knights Templar founded a preceptory here.

GUITING POWER

A couple of miles downstream, Temple Guiting's sister village, Guiting Power, is a delightful collection of Cotswold stone cottages clustered around a triangular green. In the 1970s, Richard Cochrane, a local property owner who had acquired around half the cottages in the village, set up a trust to ensure that housing would continue to be offered to local people at affordable rents. This scheme has also helped to preserve the rural character of the village, with its steep gables, mullioned windows and neat blue doors. Other noteworthy features here are the part-Norman **St Michael's Church**, the First World War memorial cross, and the old bakery in Well Lane which has an unusual columned frontage dating back to the early 17th century.

Midway between the Guitings, the 1000 acre **Cotswold Farm Park** is a characteristic Cotswolds hill farm which contains one of the largest collections of rare British farm animals in the country. Visitors are encouraged to meet the animals which include longhorn cattle, Gloucester Old Spot pigs, and a local breed of thickly-fleeced sheep known as Cotswold Lions. Many foals, calves and lambs are born at the farm throughout the year, and there is also an adventure playground, pets corner, café and farm trail. (Open daily, 11am to 5pm between April and end-September.)

The lanes to the west of the Guitings cross the **Salt Way**, an ancient packhorse trail which runs along the ridge between the Windrush valley and the vale of Sudeley. Because of the lack of winter foodstuffs, it was a common medieval practice to slaughter livestock in the autumn and then preserve the meat in barrels of salt. The mineral became a valuable commodity and a network of routes grew up between its source (in this case Droitwich in Worcestershire) and the rest of the country. The most accessible section of the Cotswolds Salt Way runs for seven miles south from Hailes Abbey to a point on the A436 three miles east of Andoversford. Near its northern end, the route passes close to Salter's Hill, an impressive viewpoint lying two miles east of Winchcombe.

WINCHCOMBE

To the west of the Salt Way, and to the southeast of Winchcombe, lies **Sudeley Castle**, a restored medieval stately home which provides a fascinating day out for visitors of all ages. The castle is perhaps best known as the burial place of Catherine Parr, the sixth and last wife of Henry VIII. After outliving Henry, she married her former lover, Sir Thomas Seymour, Baron of Sudeley, but sadly died in childbirth the following year. Catherine's marble tomb can be seen in **St Mary's Chapel**; however, this is not the original but a 19th century replacement designed by Sir Gilbert Scott to take the place of the one destroyed during the English Civil War. Sudeley Castle was a Royalist stronghold during that war and was twice besieged, once in 1643 and again in 1644. The conflict left the castle damaged by cannon fire and a large gap can still be seen in the wall of the Octagon Tower.

During the following two centuries, Sudeley was badly neglected and much of the stone was carted away by the local inhabitants for use as building material; indeed, by the 1820s, it had degenerated into a common alehouse, the Castle Arms. It wasn't until 1837 that the castle and 60 acres of land were rescued by the Dent family. Emma Dent was responsible for the impressive period restoration of the exterior and for refurbishing the interior in sumptuous Victorian style. She also accumulated a large number of now-priceless old masters, including work by Constable, Turner, Van Dyck and Rubens, as well as a superb collection of tapestries, period furniture, costumes and one of the largest private collections of toys in Europe. Visitors are now able to view the magnificent interior and walk around Sudeley's extensive grounds which contain a lake, a formal garden and a famous 15ft double yew hedge. A more recent addition has been a large adventure playground complete with replica castle. (Open daily, 12 noon to 5pm between 1 April and 31 October.)

Sudeley Castle, Winchcombe Tel: 01242 602308

The attractive small town of Winchcombe was once a regional capital of Saxon Mercia. One of the town's more enduring legends concerns, Kenelm, a popular child king who is said to have been martyred here by his jealous sister, Quendrida, in the 8th century. As a way of calming a mob of people who had gathered to voice their disapproval at this murderous act, legend has it that she recited Psalm 109 backwards, a deed which resulted in her being struck blind in an act of divine retribution.

In medieval times, St Kenelm's shrine grew to rank second only to Thomas à Becket's as a place of pilgrimage and as a result, the town became one of the foremost tourist destinations of its day. Winchcombe grew to become a walled town with an abbot who presided over a Saxon parliament. However in 1539, the abbey was destroyed by Thomas Seymour of Sudeley following Henry VIII's Dissolution of the Monasteries. All that remains of it today is a section of a gallery which is now part of the George Inn.

Following the destruction of the abbey, the local people were forced to find an alternative source of income. This they found in a new crop which had just been introduced from the New World - tobacco. Despite the vagaries of the English climate, for several decades Winchcombe earned a healthy living out of this increasingly popular cash crop, something which is reflected in a variety of present day place names, including Tobacco Close and Tobacco Field.

Winchcombe's new found prosperity was brought to an abrupt end in 1670 when an act of Parliament banned home-produced tobacco in favour of imports from the struggling colony of Virginia. Thanks to the long period of decline which followed this legislative interference, the town has been left with a great many unaltered early buildings.

These include the splendid parish church, with its 40 leering gargoyles and an altar cloth reputed to have been embroidered by Catherine of Aragon, and a group of fine Tudor houses in Hailes Street.

Hailes Street is also the location of **Petticoat Tails**, a truly delightful place to enjoy a delicious morning coffee, lunch, afternoon tea or early evening meal. This fully licensed tearoom and restaurant is run by mother and daughter Jean Scholes and Lorraine Waterson. All their scones are baked fresh each morning, and their cakes are home-made from their own unique recipes. They also serve delicious home-cooked lunches, and in summer, an evening bistro menu which features such imaginative dishes as blackened chicken in pineapple salsa. Customers can sit inside, or in the tea garden with its fabulous view of the Cotswold Way.

Petticoat Tails
7 Hailes Street
Winchcombe
Tel: 01242 603578

Barbecues are held on Sunday nights in fine weather.

The White Hart, High Street, Winchcombe Tel: 01242 602359

One of the oldest inns in Winchcombe, the **White Hart** is a splendid pub, restaurant and place to stay which is easily located in the High Street. This impressive part-timbered building has a private car park to the rear and for much of the year is decked in a wonderful floral display. Inside, it has lost none of its original character, with oak-beamed ceilings, open fires and an interesting collection of horse racing memorabilia, including several antique saddles.

Proprietors Mari and Alistair MacPherson offer a fine selection of traditional ales and an extensive bar meals menu, with dishes ranging from sandwiches and jacket potatoes to steaks and chicken Kiev. With its seven beautifully appointed en-suite guest bedrooms, the White Hart also provides an excellent base for exploring the Cotswolds. Guests are invited to make use of the inn's snooker cellar and games room, although they should keep an eye open for the friendly ghost which is apt pay a visit from time to time.

Plaisterers Arms, Abbey Terrace, Winchcombe Tel: 01242 602358

In the centre of Winchcombe is a fine inn, the **Plaisterers Arms**. Dating from the 18th century, this impressive establishment has oak-beamed ceilings and a wonderful traditional atmosphere. Landlord David Gould serves a range of hand-pulled ales and an excellent selection of bar meals, including delicious homemade pies and traditional roast lunch on Sundays. He also has five comfortable guest rooms available which are all equipped with en-suite facilities.

To the rear, the land slopes away sharply to form a delightful beer garden. An attractive patio area has been created here, and in summer the whole area overflows with spectacular floral displays. The garden enjoys fine views over the surrounding landscape and also contains a large children's play area. Children are also very welcome in the pub's dining area. One of several interesting specialist museums in the town, the **Winchcombe Folk and Police Museum** is situated adjacent to the tourist information centre in the town hall. As well as information on the history of the town from neolithic times to the recent past, it also contains an intriguing collection of police equipment and uniforms, both from British and overseas forces. (Open Mondays to Saturdays, 10am to 5pm between 1 April and 31 October.)

Ireley Farm, Broadway Road, Winchcombe Tel: 01242 602445

Those wishing to stay in the relaxed atmosphere of farmhouse accommodation should make a point of finding **Ireley Farm**, a delightful bed and breakfast establishment which is run by Margaret and Ian Warmington. Situated just off the Broadway road on the edge of Winchcombe, the farm has a history going back to Roman and medieval times. It is set around an elegant 18th century residence built of golden

Cotswold limestone which stands within 500 acres of beautiful rolling farmland. Inside, the house has a handsome panelled hallway, open fires and three spacious guest bedrooms, all oak-beamed and decorated in charming country style. Maggie and Ian provide the warmest of welcomes and a delicious farmhouse breakfast. Horse riding and rough shooting are also available nearby.

An ordinary looking Victorian house is the home of the fascinating **Winchcombe Railway Museum and Garden**. Tim Petchey has spent decades assembling his superb collection of signalling equipment, lineside notices and railway memorabilia, much of which adorns his beautiful half acre garden. There is also a working signal box, a booking office and a large display of printed railway ephemera, including tickets and posters. A mecca for all steam railway enthusiasts, this absorbing museum lies hidden down a narrow passageway in Gloucester Street. (Open 1.30pm to 5.30pm; please telephone for current opening programme.)

Winchcombe Railway Museum, 23 Gloucester Street, Winchcombe
Tel: 01242 620641

Also to be found on the Broadway Road on the northern outskirts of Winchcombe is the **Winchcombe Pottery**. Established in 1926 on the site of an old rural pottery works dating back to the 1800s, this impressive working pottery has been in the same family for over 60 years.

Winchcombe Pottery Ltd,
Broadway Road,
Winchcombe
Tel: 01242 602462

Between 1926 and the early 1950s it produced domestic slipware fired in a bottle kiln which is still in existence, but is not now in use. The work produced today includes a wide range of hand-thrown domestic stoneware which is fired to about 1300°C in a wood-fired down-draught kiln. Stoneware is hard, durable and entirely free from lead or any injurious chemicals, so it is kind to the environment as well as looking great.

Visitors are welcome to tour the showroom and, at most times, the workshop where they can view these wonderful pieces being produced by hand. As well as the standard range of domestic ware, Winchcombe Pottery also produces a number of individual items which are offered in the showroom at competitive prices. A furniture maker and sculptor also share the premises, making this a haven for collectors of fine local art and crafts.

Ireley Grounds, the new home of the renowned Barnhouse Catering Company, is a stunning Cotswold farmhouse set in two-and-a-half acres of beautiful grounds beside the B4632 Winchcombe to Broadway road. A place that can cater for every requirement, large or small, Ireley provides one of the most stylish and original venues for weddings and private parties in the Cotswolds. The lounge, with its sofas, log fire and solid oak bar, has plenty of style and atmosphere, whilst the three main bedroom suites are beautifully furnished with all the usual facilities; one of the most luxurious rooms even has a romantic four-poster bed. Some excellent cottage-style overnight accommodation is also available on a self-catering basis, although with the Barnhouse Catering Company just a few steps away, guests won't need to do much of their own cooking!

Ireley Grounds, Broadway Road, Winchcombe Tel: 01242 603736

Ireley also offers sports facilities and other entertainments, such as clay pigeon shooting and magnificent medieval banquets. The gardens of Ireley are spectacular. Thanks to the devoted efforts of Mike and Pauline, the grounds are a riot of colour all year round. In spring, the rhododendrons come to life in a brilliant display of colour, whilst the beautiful Koi pond adds a distinctive aquatic feel to this delightful garden. With the Gloucestershire-Warwickshire steam railway running across the bottom of the grounds and some breathtaking views of the surrounding landscape, Ireley Grounds are perfect for that special break in the Cotswold countryside.

The National Trust-owned **Hailes Abbey** is situated a mile-and-a-half to the northeast of Winchcombe. Now largely ruined, the monastery was founded in 1246 by Richard, Earl of Cornwall following his narrow escape from a shipwreck off the Scilly Isles. Unfortunately, it was built to such an ambitious scale that the Cistercian monks found it difficult to maintain financially, at least until a wealthy patron donated a phial which was claimed to contain the blood of Jesus Christ. Thanks to this holy relic, the abbey soon became one of Europe's most important places of pilgrimage and was even referred to in Chaucer's *Canterbury Tales*.

Hailes Abbey

This boom in the fortunes of Hailes Abbey lasted until the Dissolution of the Monasteries in 1539 when the authenticity of the relic was questioned and the phial destroyed. The abbey then fell into disrepair and today, the only significant parts to survive are seventeen arches of the monastic cloister. A large number of artefacts have been found on the site, including medieval floor tiles and fragments of elaborate stone sculptures, and these are now on display in an interesting museum which is open daily, 10am to 6pm between 1 April and end-October, and Wednesdays to Sundays, 10am to 4pm in winter.

The nearby parish church of Hailes was constructed around 1130 and predates the abbey. Many of the floor tiles once belonged to the abbey and were transferred here following the Dissolution. There are also some fine 14th century wall paintings and a canopied pulpit dating from the 1600s.

STANWAY

Stanway House, Stanway Tel: 01386 584469

This is a charming village which lies tucked under the Cotswolds ridge a couple of miles to the north of Winchcombe. The view down to the village from the B4077 on the escarpment above is one of the loveliest in Gloucestershire. Stanway itself contains a number of interesting architectural features including a 14th century medieval tithe barn, an unusual bronze of St George on the war memorial, and private cricket pavilion built on curious mushroom-shaped staddle-stones.

An ornate Jacobean gatehouse guards the entrance to **Stanway House**, a beautiful country mansion built of mellow honey-gold Cotswold limestone which is one of the finest examples of its kind in the county. This outstanding Jacobean squire's manor house was built between 1580 and 1640 by the Tracys of Stanway, a landed family who had owned property in Gloucestershire since pre-Norman times. Other than by inheritance, the estate has only changed hands once in the last 1250 years. Today, Stanway is still very much the family home of Lord Neidpath, who has personally written an excellent guide to the house which is available to visitors to help them enjoy their tour around the property. It is also a pleasure to read the guide afterwards, when it helps to refresh the memory of the many delights of the house.

The gatehouse, which stands between the church and the main house, was built around 1630, it was believed, by Inigo Jones, though more recently it has been ascribed to Timothy Strong of Barrington. One of the gems of Cotswold architecture, an interesting piece of history is connected with the scallop shells which adorn its walls. Sir William de Traci of Barnstaple was one of the four knights who murdered St Thomas á Becket in Canterbury Cathedral at the instigation of Henry II. After the King repented of this horrendous crime, Sir William was obliged to make a pilgrimage to Jerusalem, and so, it is supposed, the Tracys adopted the scallop shell crest of St James of Compostella, the patron saint of pilgrims.

The shuffleboard table along the west wall of the hall was built about 1620. The game, an early form of shove-halfpenny, was very popular in the 16th and 17th centuries. There are only three in existence known to be in full working order complete with their brass counters, so this is a rare example indeed. It is particularly special because it has a single piece of oak as the playing surface. In the bay window there is a Chippendale exercising chair; at one time, vigorous bouncing on this for half-an-hour a day was considered good for the health. There are also two fine Broadwood pianos which, despite having once lain neglected in an unheated, unlit, unventilated and uninhabited room, have remained in excellent condition.

Stanway House is filled with fine paintings, many of them portraits of family ancestors, which add to the atmosphere of this lovely house. Stanway is also known for being the home of Thomas Dover, the sea captain who rescued Alexander Selkirk from a deserted island, an event which was to give Daniel Defoe the inspiration to write *Robinson Crusoe*. The house stands in extensive landscaped grounds containing a medieval tithe bar, water mill, ice house, brewery, dog's cemetery, and a curious 18th century pyramid. (Open Tuesdays and Thursdays, 2pm to 5pm between June and end-September.)

STANTON

Stanway's sister village, Stanton, lies a mile further north. This attractive Cotswold village consists almost entirely of steeply-gabled limestone cottages built during the 16th and 17th centuries. One of the reasons Stanton is so well preserved is that it was owned by the architect Sir Philip Stott between 1906 and 1937. Stott's home, **Stanton Court**, is an elegant Jacobean residence which was built by the Chamberlain to Queen Elizabeth I when the original 16th century manor, Warren Farm House, had become outmoded. The house is set within beautiful landscaped grounds which are occasionally open to the public on summer Sundays.

Stanton Court Cottages, Stanton, Near Broadway
Tel: 01386 584551 Fax: 01386 584682

Attached to Stanton Court are the superb **Stanton Court Cottages**, eight top-class self-catering holiday cottages which were built of local Cotswold limestone in the 16th and 17th centuries. Now luxuriously renovated, they provide the ideal place to completely unwind and get away from the daily trials of life. The cottages are set around a wonderful old courtyard within five acres of impressive landscaped gardens containing orchards, sweeping lawns and beautifully-kept flower beds. The grounds also contain an adventure playground, a heated outdoor swimming pool (open in summer), a tennis court (open weekdays), and a games room containing a pool table, table tennis, darts and table football.

Stanton Court Cottages sleep from two to seven people and are appointed to an extremely high standard. All have full gas central heating, direct-dial telephones, fully-equipped modern fitted kitchens, attractively decorated dining/sitting areas with colour TV, modern bathrooms with showers and plenty of hot water, and bedrooms with all linen and continental quilts provided. There are also excellent on-site laundry facilities. Open all year, the cottages are luxurious and stylish, yet comfortable and informal, and provide the ideal environment in which to relax and enjoy the beautiful surroundings and many nearby places of interest.

The Vine, Stanton, Near Broadway Tel: 01386 584250
Fax: 01386 584385

First-rate accommodation in Stanton village is offered by Jill Gabb at her substantial 17th century stone-built farmhouse, **The Vine**. Lying just to the east of the B4632 between Winchcombe and Broadway, this exceptional family run bed and breakfast establishment can also be reached on foot via the Cotswolds Way. It stands within a beautiful low-walled garden and was once the home of the local bailiff. The atmosphere is warm and friendly with open log fires, a superb dining room and three spacious guest bedrooms, each with a four-poster bed. Mrs Gabb also runs the nearby riding stables and provides qualified instruction in show jumping, hunting and dressage to all levels. She is happy to accommodate unaccompanied children, and adults who come to ride with the North Cotswolds Hunt.

Stanton's village **Church of St Michael's and All Angels** has a number of interesting features including a fine Perpendicular south aisle and porch, an east window which contains stained glass from the ruined abbey at Hailes, and a number of medieval pews whose deeply scarred ends have been attributed to the leashes of dogs belonging to local shepherds. A number of early 20th century additions were made to the church by the architect Sir Ninian Comper, including the organ loft, the rood screen and a number of stained-glass windows whose designer can be identified by a distinctive wild strawberry.

TODDINGTON

The northern terminus of the privately-owned **Gloucestershire-Warwickshire Railway** is situated close to the junction of the B4632 and B4077, one-and-a-half miles south of Stanton. From the restored Toddington station it is possible to take a steam train for an enjoyable six mile return trip through some of the loveliest countryside in Gloucestershire. The restored Great Western Railway station is open to the public all year round and includes a signal box and a goods shed. Train trips at an extra charge depart between 12 noon and 5pm on Saturdays and Sundays between March and October. A mile or so to the west of Toddington Station, it's worth turning north off the B4077 Tewkesbury road to visit the village of Toddington itself.

GRETTON

Situated on the outskirts of Gretton near the western terminus of the Gloucestershire-Warwickshire Railway, **Elms Farm** is a 120 acre modern working farm, with sheep, cereals and extensive mushroom-growing tunnels, which also offers charming farmhouse accommodation. Guests are invited to walk around the farm, or join the many public footpaths which crisscross the area. The farm is well looked after and offers a peaceful location where children are safe to enjoy the animals at close hand. The bedrooms all have en-suite facilities and picturesque views over the surrounding landscape. A delicious English farmhouse breakfast is a tempting prospect, even for the dieters, and evening meals can be provided by arrangement. English Tourist Board 2 crown commended, Elms Farm lies a mile from the famous Prescott Hill Climb, and Sudeley Castle and the historic town of Winchcombe are just two miles away.

Elms Farm, Gretton, Near Winchcombe Tel: 01242 620150

LITTLE WASHBOURNE

The charming settlement of Little Washbourne lies in the lanes a couple of miles to the northwest of Gretton, in a broad valley which sweeps down from the Cotswolds to the River Severn. **Bredon Hill**, an upland area to the northwest of here, is a spur of the Cotswolds which extends across the Hereford and Worcester border.

TEWKESBURY

From Bredon Hill, it is only a short journey back across the Gloucestershire border to Tewkesbury, a historic and strategically important town which stands at the confluence of the rivers Severn and Avon. Because its position between the two rivers prevented it from expanding outwards, Tewkesbury's narrow streets became densely packed with unusually tall buildings, many of which were constructed during a time of prosperity in the 15th and 16th centuries. Thanks to the period of relative decline which followed, a great many handsome black-and-white timber-framed structures remain. Today, these are best seen on foot.

Tewkesbury's three main thoroughfares, the High Street, Church Street and Barton Street, form a 'Y' shape, and the area between is filled with narrow alleyways and hidden courtyards which contain some wonderful old pubs and medieval cottages. At the centre of the 'Y' stands the spectacular **Tewkesbury Abbey**, a parish church of cathedral-like proportions which was founded in the 8th century and completely rebuilt at the end of the 11th century. It was once the church of the mighty Benedictine Abbey of Tewkesbury and was one of the last monasteries to be dissolved by Henry VIII. In 1540, it was saved from destruction by the town burghers who bought it from the crown for just £453.

One of its most striking internal features is the colossal double row of Norman pillars. These support some fine early 14th century roof vaulting which in recent years has been restored to its original colour. In the central choir, there are seven superb stained-glass windows incorporating glass dating from the 14th century. Two other outstanding features are the abbey's Milton organ, whose early 17th century pipes are thought to be some of the oldest in the country still in regular use, and the high altar, which consists of a massive single slab of Purbeck marble over 13 feet in length.

At 132 feet high and 46 feet square, Tewkesbury Abbey's colossal main tower is believed to be the largest Norman church tower still in existence. Those making the climb to the top will be rewarded with a breathtaking view of the town and the surrounding landscape. Indeed, the tower was used as a lookout position during one of the bloodiest and most decisive confrontations of the Wars of the Roses, the Battle of Tewkesbury.

The battle took place on Saturday 4 May 1471 in a field to the south of the town which ever since has been known as Bloody Meadow. Following the Lancastrian defeat, those who had not been slaughtered on the battlefield fled to the abbey where they were pursued by the victorious Yorkist army. A further massacre began, but this was halted by timely intervention of Abbot Strensham. Two days later, however, the refugees, who included the Duke of Somerset, were handed over to the king and executed at the town's Market Cross. The seventeen year old son of Henry VI, Edward Prince of Wales, was also killed during the conflict and a plaque marking his final resting place can be seen in the abbey.

Tewkesbury

Almost two centuries later, Tewkesbury was again the scene of military action, this time during the English Civil War. The town changed hands several times during the conflict and on one occasion, Charles I began his siege of Gloucester by requisitioning every pick, mattock, spade and shovel in Tewkesbury.

Those keen on finding out more about the town's turbulent military history should follow the **Tewkesbury's Battle Trail**. An informative guide for this interesting walk is available at the Tourist Information Office. Alternatively, there is an impressive model of the battlefield in the **Tewkesbury Town Museum**. This excellent museum occupies a medieval timber-framed building in Barton Street and contains a number of displays on the social history and archeology of Tewkesbury and its environs. (Open daily, 10am to 1pm and 2pm to 5pm between Easter and end-October.)

Collections, 5 Barton Street, Tewkesbury
Tel: 01684 290775/298708

Lying within easy reach of the museum in Barton Street, **Collections** is a wonderful Aladdin's cave, both for the casual browser and the serious collector of historic ephemera. Conveniently situated near the Cross, this fascinating shop contains a staggering variety of rare collectibles, including Victorian and Edwardian postcards, cigarette cards (both odds and complete sets), British and Commonwealth stamps, Victorian scraps and greeting cards, advertising material, militaria, and rare books and records. Knowledgeable and welcoming, proprietors Chris and Roy Evans also specialise in unique one-twelfth scale Dandelion Dolls. They manufacture their own dolls' furniture and also offer an efficient in-house photographic and framing service.

Two specialist museums can be found almost adjacent to each other in Church Street. The **Little Museum** is situated in a timber-framed merchant's house dating from around 1450. The building was fully restored in 1971 and is laid out as a recreation of a typical Tewkesbury merchant's home and workplace during the late medieval period. (Open

Tuesdays to Saturdays and Bank Holiday Mondays, 10am to 5pm between Easter and October; admission free.)

The nearby **John Moore Countryside Museum** contains a wide variety of artefacts relating to the Gloucestershire countryside, past and present. It was opened in 1980 in commemoration of the work of John Moore, a well-known local writer, broadcaster and natural history enthusiast who was born in Tewkesbury in 1907. Items on show include agricultural implements, domestic equipment and a wide range of rural memorabilia. The museum set out to be particularly appealing to children and is also concerned with local nature conservation. (Open Tuesdays to Saturdays and Bank Holiday Mondays, 10am to 1pm and 2pm to 5pm between Easter and October.)

Aardvark (Crafts and Gifts), 9 Church Street, Tewkesbury
Tel: 01684 299339

Also in Church Street in the heart of old Tewkesbury, one of the most imaginative ranges of gifts and crafts in north Gloucestershire can be found at **Aardvark (Crafts and Gifts)**, a delightful 15th century building which is noted for its unusual frescoed windows. Here, Amanda Thomas has assembled a superb collection of gift ideas, including jewellery,

Belgian chocolates, toys, wind chimes, mobiles, novelty doormats and handicrafts from around the world. She also stocks a wide selection of locally-made crafts and souvenirs of the Tewkesbury area, all beautifully laid out in a constantly changing display. Aardvark also offers black and white and colour photocopying, and a fax service.

Tewkesbury also has some renowned literary associations. Charles Dickens set part of *The Pickwick Papers* in the town's Royal Hop Pole Hotel, and the Victorian romantic writer, Mrs Craik, based her novel *John Halifax, Gentleman* on the people and places of the borough.

FORTHAMPTON

The unspoilt Severn Vale village of **FORTHAMPTON** lies across the River Severn, three miles to the west of Tewkesbury. This attractive collection of 16th and 17th century timber-framed farmhouses and cottages are loosely grouped around a knoll which is surmounted by the part 13th century **Church of St Mary**. The narrow lanes are lined with beautiful old buildings, including the Sanctuary, with its 15th century great hall, the imposing 18th century **Forthampton House**, and the similarly-aged **Southfield House** with its distinctive brick-built dovecote. The grounds of Southfield House contain the former country retreat of the abbots of Tewkesbury, Forthampton Court, and are occasionally open to the public.

DEERHURST

The attractive hamlet of Deerhurst is situated on the eastern bank of the Severn, two miles to the southwest of Tewkesbury. The small size of the present day village disguises the fact that in Saxon times, it was of much greater importance. Indeed, this was once the site of the most powerful monastery in Hwicce, the Anglo-Saxon principality of the lower Severn.

The **Church** is one of the oldest in Britain and has parts dating back to the 7th century, the period the monastery would have been at the height of its influence. The building has a distinct Celtic feel and contains a number of surprising features. The elaborate double east window is unique to Deerhurst and is considered to bear more of a resemblance to a window in Ethiopia's Debra Damo monastery than it does to any equivalent construction in Britain. There are also some unusual Saxon carvings, including an angel in the apse which probably dates from the 9th century, and an exceptionally fine carved font which was found buried in a local farmyard. This is also 9th century and is carved with a Celtic trumpet spiral, a vine scroll and an unusual Northumbrian motif. The present base has different origins and originally belonged to a carved Saxon cross.

St Alphege, who went on to become Archbishop of Canterbury and was eventually martyred by the Danes, was a monk here during the 10th century, and some decades later, King Edmund Ironside of the Saxons signed a treaty of cooperation with Canute, King of the Danes on a nearby island in the Severn. The church also contains a number of 14th century memorial brasses commemorating the Cassey family, owners of the estate to the south which now encompasses the handsome 16th century Wightfield Manor.

The floor of nearby Abbots Court once concealed the remains **Odda's Chapel**, another Saxon treasure which was founded in 1056 by the Earl Odda, a trusted friend of Edward the Confessor. A stone inscribed with the date of consecration was discovered in 1675 and is now on view in the Ashmolean Museum in Oxford. A copy of this Odda Stone can be seen inside the chapel which is now administered by English Heritage and is open to the public.

CHELTENHAM

A six mile drive to the southeast of Deerhurst leads to the superb Georgian town of Cheltenham, one of the largest centres of population in Gloucestershire. Unlike most other settlements we have so far visited, Cheltenham's history is a relatively short one. Indeed, the only surviving medieval building here is the parish **Church of St Mary** in Clarence Street, which has parts dating back to the 12th century. This is worth a visit, partly to make a comparison with the rest of the town, and partly to view its fine stained-glass windows. The most renowned of these is the circular east window which has some exceptionally delicate 14th century tracery. Look out also for the unusual 13th century Sanctus bell in the chancel.

Prior to the 18th century, Cheltenham was a small market town with a single main street. However in 1715, a local farmer accidentally discovered a saline spring in one of his fields, an occurrence which began a sequence of events which was to change the character of Cheltenham out of all recognition. Twenty years later, his son-in-law, the retired privateer Captain Henry Skillicorne, saw the potential of the discovery and built an enclosure around the spring, along with a meeting room, a ballroom, and a network of walks and rides which now form the tree-lined Promenade. Later, he added a stylish Long Room to the complex of buildings.

As the reputation of Cheltenham Spa grew, a number of other springs were discovered, including one in the High Street around which the first Assembly Rooms were constructed. In 1788, the prosperity of the town was assured following the visit of George III who, along with his queen and daughters, spent five weeks in Cheltenham taking the waters. This royal endorsement made the town a highly fashionable resort and a period of spectacular development followed. A team of eminent architects were commissioned to plan an entirely new town which would incorporate the best features of neoclassical Regency architecture, a scheme which turned out to be so successful that it attracted many prominent figures of the day, including the Duke of Wellington who spent several weeks in Cheltenham in 1816 treating a liver complaint he had contracted in the Tropics.

The Promenade, Cheltenham

This golden era of architecture reached its high point in the late 1820s with the completion of two unique structures. The Promenade is noted for its superb fountain of Neptune, and the Pittville Pump Room is an extravagant masterpiece which stands within spacious parkland to the north of the town centre. The latter was designed by John Forbes and features a great hall fronted by a colonnade of Ionic columns and topped by a domed gallery. It was built by Joseph Pitt MP as a place to entertain his circle of friends, though by the time of his death in 1842, the cost of its construction had left him heavily in debt.

Today, the building houses the **Pittville Pump Room Museum**, an imaginative museum of original period costume which brings to life Cheltenham's past from its Regency renaissance to the swinging 1960s. There is also an interesting display of rare jewellery and tiaras which chronicle the changes in fashion that occurred between the Regency and Art Nouveau periods. A series of special exhibitions is held throughout the year. (Open Tuesday to Saturdays (also summer Sundays and Bank Holiday Mondays), 10am to 4.30pm, all year round.)

The **Willoughby House Hotel** is a magnificent star-listed Regency hotel which is situated just a few minutes walk from the centre of Cheltenham. Once a private home which welcomed members of the royal family through its imposing entrance, Willoughby House has been tastefully converted into a hotel and apartments which offer homely comforts and outstanding value for money. There are eight light and airy en-suite guest rooms, each individually styled and furnished in luxurious fabrics and furnishings. The rooms range from a beautiful suite complete with four-poster bed, adjoining second bedroom and lounge area, to family doubles, twins and single rooms. All the guest rooms have tea and coffee making facilities, TVs, direct-dial telephones and room service.

Breakfast and dinner are served in the dining room of Willoughby House which is beautifully decorated in sunny, warm colours. This elegant room boasts stunning views of the extensive gardens, as do the equally impressive guest lounge and library. The food at the hotel restaurant is widely acclaimed for its high quality and freshness. The extensive and regularly-changing dinner menu includes such starters as French onion tartlets served warm with a piquant tomato sauce, and main courses such as 10oz fillet steak finished in either a balsamic vinegar or Stilton glaze. Those with room for dessert should try the chilled fresh raspberry soufflé which is absolutely superb.

*Willoughby House Hotel, 1 Suffolk Square, Cheltenham
Tel: 01242 522798*

In addition to the guest rooms, Willoughby House also offers three totally self-contained apartments, each with its own entrance. The coach house is detached from the main building and is newlyconverted from the old stable block and groom's quarters. It offers a lounge with all the usual facilities, fully-fitted kitchen, bathroom, laundry and second WC, and two twin bedrooms. The sofa in the lounge also converts to a double bed, so the house will comfortably sleep six. The maisonette and the garden flat each sleep four and offer the same level of comfort and style. The central location of Willoughby House also makes it an ideal business base. The management welcome meetings of up to twenty people, and provide excellent phone, fax and catering facilities at competitive rates.

Two worthwhile museums are situated near the centre of Cheltenham. The **Gustav Holst Birthplace Museum** in Clarence Road is housed in the terraced Regency house where the famous composer of the *Planets Suite* was born in 1874. Among the items on show is Holst's original concert piano. The house has been refurbished in keeping with the 'upstairs-downstairs' way of life which would have prevailed in the late-Victorian era and includes a gracious Regency drawing room, a children's nursery filled with period memorabilia, and a working kitchen with a housekeeper's room, pantry, scullery and laundry. (Open Tuesdays to Saturdays, 10am to 4.30pm, all year round.)

The **Cheltenham Art Gallery and Museum** in Clarence Street is also worth a visit, especially by those interested in furniture and silver. The museum has a fine collection of Cotswold-made pieces inspired by William Morris, the Pre-Raphaelite artist and poet who founded the much respected Arts and Crafts Movement in the 19th century. Other work on show includes an impressive display of oriental porcelain, English ceramics, pewter, glassware and a permanent collection of paintings by Dutch and British masters. There is also a fascinating collection of personal items belonging to Edward Wilson, a member of Captain Scott's ill-fated team of Antarctic explorers. (Open Mondays to Saturdays, 10am to 5.30pm, all year round and on Sunday afternoons in June, July and August (closed Bank Holidays); admission free.)

Present day Cheltenham continues to attract visitors to its elegant Georgian streets. Best explored on foot, these include Suffolk Place, Lansdown Place and Montpelier Walk. One of the common features of the architecture is the delicate ironwork which is built into many of the upstairs balconies and verandas. Cheltenham's famous spa water can still be sampled at the town hall and the Pittville Pump Room. Said to be the only naturally occurring alkaline spring water in the country, it is believed to be instilled with beneficial medicinal properties. It certainly is an acquired taste.

The charming **Milton House Hotel** is situated in the very heart of picturesque Cheltenham. Owned and run by Penny and Alex, this stunning Regency house was sympathetically restored in 1983 and still retains a distinct air of elegance and luxury. Each of the eight guest rooms has its own character and style, and is finished with those extra touches that make a stay not only enjoyable but memorable. All bedrooms are equipped with en-suite facilities, beverage trays, satellite TVs, direct-dial telephones, radio alarm clocks and hair dryers.

Milton House's Regency lounge is delightfully restful, just the place for a read or a quiet chat, and there is also an elegant sun lounge and bar with a more intimate atmosphere which overlooks the garden to the rear. The dining room fills with early morning sun and is the perfect spot to enjoy a delicious breakfast. The car park in Royal Parade Mews, a quiet cul-de-sac, is only a few paces from the boutiques and antique shops of

Montpelier, one of the most interesting shopping centres in the country. A small hotel with a friendly atmosphere, excellent service and a feeling of quality, Milton House is a place to return to time and time again.

Milton House Hotel, 12 Royal Parade, Bayshill Road, Cheltenham
Tel: 01242 582601

Each year, Cheltenham hosts a number of top-class arts festivals. In May, a two week Festival of Music, Speech, Drama and Dance is held; this is followed in July by the International Festival of Music, which features a wide variety of classical concerts, opera and recitals; then in October, the Festival of Literature features readings, exhibitions and a range of literary events. The Everyman Theatre, Cheltenham's former opera house, provides a first-rate venue for performed work of all kinds.

A popular Cricket Festival has been held in Cheltenham each August since 1877, and the town also hosts one of the nation's premier horse racing events, the Cheltenham National Hunt Festival, which takes place in March. Cheltenham Racecourse, Britain's top steeplechasing venue, is situated at Prestbury Park, two miles north of the town centre and a little to the east of the A435.

PRESTBURY

The nearby village of Prestbury contains an abundance of thatched timber-framed buildings, two welcoming pubs, and the lost remains of a medieval bishop's palace. It is also inhabited by an unusually large and colourful selection of ghosts, including Old Moses the groom, a young woman playing the spinet, a lone strangler, a black abbot, and a man on a bicycle.

CLEEVE HILL

A spectacular view of Cheltenham and the surrounding landscape can be obtained from Cleeve Cloud, which at 1083 feet above sea level is the highest point in the Cotswolds. The summit is situated four miles northeast of Cheltenham and can be reached by walking southeast along the Cotswolds Way for just over a mile from the village of Cleeve Hill. The view from the Cotswolds ridge is breathtaking, with Tewkesbury Abbey, the Herefordshire Beacon and the distant Brecon Beacons all being visible on a clear day.

One of the finest examples of a neolithic long barrow can be found a couple of miles along the ridge to the east of Cleeve Cloud (it can either be approached from Cleeve Hill or from the village of Charlton Abbots). Known as **Belas Knap**, the massive grass-covered barrow measures 180 feet by 60 feet and was constructed by New Stone Age people around 5000 years ago. Excavators discovered four burial chambers which together contained the remains of over 30 people. One of the most unusual features of Belas Knap is its false entrance at the broader northern end. The nearby hidden chamber was found to contain the remains of a man and five children who appeared to have been buried as part of some ancient sacrificial rite.

LECKHAMPTON

Another dramatic hilltop site can be found two-and-a-half miles south of Cheltenham, just to the east of the B4070 Birdlip road. **Leckhampton Hill** is an imposing limestone crag with a bare cliff face and a grassy crest on which an Iron Age fortification once stood. Evidence of more recent Roman and Saxon occupation has also been found here. Just below the summit stands the slender rock column known as the **Devil's Chimney** which is said to have been 'sent straight from hell'. The hill is best approached from the north along a path which rises sharply from the

B4070. After some distance this divides, offering the choice of a direct route to the top or a circular route around the summit to the west which allows a spectacular view of the Devil's Chimney.

Much of the fine limestone which was used to face Cheltenham's splendid Regency buildings was quarried at or around Leckhampton Hill, and the old quarry workings add to the rugged character of the landscape. Leckhampton village has a 14th century manor house and a church of a similar age which contains some unusual brass monuments.

The **Cotswolds Way** winds southwest from Leckhampton Hill following the exposed ridge of the Cotswolds escarpment. This impressive long distance footpath offers spectacular views across the Severn Vale to the Severn bridges and Brecon Beacons to the southwest, and across the Vale of Gloucester to Bredon Hill and the Malverns to the north. This superb three mile stretch also passes a number of dramatic promontories, the first of which is **Cooper's Hill**, a nature reserve covering 137 acres which was once the site of the most extensive Iron Age fortifications in the area. The hill has been set aside as common agricultural land since the early Middle Ages and local farmers are still entitled to exercise their special commoners' rights of *estover*, the right to collect wood for fuel, and *pannage*, the right to allow pigs to feed freely.

Each year at Whitsun, Cooper's Hill is the venue of the famous and highly risky **Cheese Rolling Ceremony** where participants chase a whole cheese down the steep slope from a maypole on the ridge above. The event is thought to have originally taken place on Midsummer's Day as part of a prehistoric sun-worshipping ceremony. Sheltering in a combe half-a-mile from Cooper's Hill are the remains of **Great Witcombe Villa**, a once-grand Roman villa which had its own bath wing and some fine mosaic floors.

A little further to the southwest, evidence of occupation by Neolithic and Iron Age people has been found at **Crickley Hill**. Today, this magnificent National Trust-owned site is run as a country park in conjunction with a neighbouring tract of land owned by Gloucestershire County Council. The area is filled with unusual geological and archeological features, and a number of interesting walks are described in leaflets available at the information point. Those with an interest in geology should look out for the nearby memorial to the young geologist, Peter Hopkins, which is constructed of five different rock types that can all be found within the Cotswold and Malvern Hills.

BIRDLIP

The third viewpoint on this stretch of the Cotswold ridge, **Birdlip Hill**, is approached from the A417 through attractive mixed woodland. The famous bronze Birdlip Mirror, now in Gloucester City Museum, was found in an Iron Age burial mound known as Barrow Wake which lies just to the north of the charming community of Birdlip. One of the highest villages in Gloucestershire, Birdlip stands near the junction of the B4070 and the A417 Ermin Way, close to the point where the old Roman road descends into the Vale of Gloucester.

BROCKWORTH

At the foot of the Birdlip and Crickley hills, the Crickley Windward Vineyard at **Little Witcombe** offers free wine tastings between Easter and Christmas.

Moat House, Shurdington Road, Brockworth, Near Cheltenham
Tel: 01452 519988 Fax: 01452 519977

One mile further west, between and to the south of the thriving market towns of Cheltenham and Gloucester, **The Moat House** is a purposebuilt hotel that provides everything guests could require for a comfortable and enjoyable stay. There are 100 well furnished bedrooms, including two luxury suites, and each guest room is provided with a king-sized bed, en-suite facilities, colour TV with in-house movies, hair dryer, tea/coffee maker, and two telephone points complete with fax/computer links. Coopers Bar serves everything from a light breakfast to afternoon tea, whilst the panoramic views from Coopers Restaurant makes it the perfect place to enjoy a delicious dinner.

The Moat House also has eleven conference rooms which are equipped with a wide variety of facilities, including multi-level lighting and the very latest presentation projectors, videos and monitors. When the times comes to take a well-earned break from the pressures of the day, guests can visit Club Moativation, the hotel's very own health and fitness centre which is superbly equipped with a full gymnasium, indoor heated pool, dance studio, solarium, spa, sauna and steam room. Set in fifteen acres of beautiful countryside within easy reach of the splendid 100 mile Cotswolds Way, the Moat House is the ideal place for those wishing to combine beautiful surroundings with the luxury of a top class hotel.

CRANHAM

Returning to the top of the Cotswold escarpment, the attractive village of Cranham lies to the southwest of Birdlip, one mile west of the B4070 Stroud road. **Prinknash Abbey** (pronounced *Prinnage*) occupies two separate sites at opposite ends of a beautiful wooded estate at the western end of the village. The old abbey was built between the 14th and 16th centuries for the Benedictine monks of Gloucester Abbey, and for a short period following the Dissolution of the Monasteries it became the country retreat of the Bishops of Gloucester. After being in private hands for over 300 years, Thomas Dyer-Edwardes, a devout Roman Catholic in his declining years, gifted the property to a community of Benedictine monks who were struggling to eke out a living on Caldey Island off the south Wales' coast.

When the white-robed monks returned to Prinknash in 1928, they found a cluster of attractive honey-coloured buildings, including a fine medieval chapel with some delicate carved woodwork and stained glass. They soon realised, however, that the old buildings were unsuitable for their expanding brotherhood, and in 1939 the foundation stone for a modern abbey was laid. This new Cotswold stone structure was designed with practical simplicity in mind and was eventually completed in 1972.

Today, the monks of Prinknash are involved in a variety of commercial activities, including the production of world-renowned **Prinknash Pottery**. Visitors are invited to tour the pottery workshops, which were established following the discovery of clay deposits on the site during construction work. (Viewing gallery open daily, 10.30am to 4.30pm (2pm to 5pm Sundays), all year round.) Although the brightly coloured earthenware is not to everyone's taste, a range of other hand-crafted items are available in the abbey's gift shop, including carved woodwork, stained glass, incense, wrought ironwork and fresh produce from the home farm.

A nine acre section of the abbey grounds is run as a separately managed establishment, the **Prinknash Bird Park**. This popular attraction is home to a wide variety of free roaming peacocks, mute swans, black swans and snow geese. It also contains a number of interesting animals, including African pygmy goats and fallow deer. An attractive woodland path leads though the Golden Wood to a haunted 16th century monk's pond which is still stocked with trout. (Open daily, 10am to 5pm between Easter and October.)

SHEEPSCOMBE

The country lanes to the east of Prinknash lead to Sheepscombe, an unspoilt community of gabled Cotswold stone farmhouses and cottages. One of the first Sunday schools in the country was established here in 1780 by a local weaver. This is thought to have provided Gloucester's Robert Raikes with the inspiration for founding the national Sunday School Movement shortly after. The nearby National Trust-owned Ebworth Estate offers some fine woodland walks. Access is via public rights of way, however parking is limited.

PAINSWICK

The beautiful small town of Painswick lies beside the A46 Cheltenham to Stroud road, two miles west of Sheepscombe. Known as the Queen of the Cotswolds, this attractive community is full of characteristic pale grey cottages built of limestone quarried at Painswick Hill, one mile to the north. Between the 15th and 18th centuries, Painswick was a prosperous wool trading and cloth manufacturing centre, and a number of large merchants' houses dating from this period can be found in and

Painswick

Rococo Gardens, Painswick

around Bisley Street. The churchyard, too, is filled with elaborate table tombs, many of which describe their occupier's profession as 'clothier'.

As seen on *Wish You Were Here* and featured in *Period Living And Traditional Homes Magazine*, **Cardynham House** is an absolute hidden gem.

Positioned in the centre of Painswick, guests passing through the little entrance step back in time. Four-poster beds, beams throughout, open fires and an old bread oven all contribute to the wealth of character of this remarkable part 15th century Grade II star listed house.

All guest bedrooms have been individually decorated by the artist owner and given names such as the Dovecote, Highlands, Old Tuscany, Medieval Garden, New England and Palm Beach. Each is furnished with antique furniture, murals and garlands of dried flowers, and equipped with en-suite or private bathrooms, colour TV, clock radio and tea/coffee making

facilities. English Tourist Board 3 crowns commended, the house has central heating and a full fire certificate, and wines and spirits are also available as Cardynham House is fully licensed.

Meals, including romantic dinners by candlelight, are served in the March Hare, a delightful room with a large open fire in winter which contains a collection of antiques and collectables, many of which are for sale. Breakfast is a speciality at Cardynham House, where the extensive menu includes American pancakes, waffles and maple syrup. Morning coffee, afternoon tea and home-made cakes are served in summer and evening meals are available by arrangement.

Painswick churchyard also contains an unusual number of carefully manicured yew trees.

Cardynham House, The Cross, Painswick Tel: 01452 814006

Local legend has it that only 99 yew trees will ever grow here, the Devil having pledged to do away with any more. Some of the trees were planted as long ago as 1714 and together, this unusual collection of skillfully-clipped arches, cones and hedges forms a living sculpture garden.

Each year on the Sunday following 8 September, **St Mary's Churchyard** is the venue for the annual Clipping (or Clypping) ceremony. Here, garlanded children join hands to encircle the church before dancing around it singing hymns. Afterwards, each child receives a silver coin, a traditional Painswick bun and a slice of 'puppy dog pie', a traditional dish containing a small china dog. The church itself dates from around 1380 and contains some unusual corbels thought to represent Richard II and his queen. Its towering 172 foot spire contains a peal of twelve bells and can seen for many miles around. One of the finest views of Painswick can be had from the top of Bulls Cross to the southeast, a place known for its ghostly atmosphere which was referred to by Laurie Lee in *Cider With Rosie*.

St Mary's Church was the site of a skirmish during the English Civil war when a party of Parliamentarian soldiers came under cannon fire while sheltering here, resulting in considerable damage to the building. Earlier in the conflict, Charles I is said to have stood at the top of nearby Painswick Beacon and enquired as to the name of woodlands below. On hearing it had none, he replied, 'let it be called Paradise', a name which has stuck to this day. A month after directing the campaign to take Gloucester, he passed this way again, defeated.

The charming **Chancellor's Tea Rooms** are situated in the very centre of this picturesque village. This charming, typically English establishment is full of warmth and character, thanks to the efforts of hosts Alan and June. They serve a wonderful selection of home-baked fare throughout the day, and also cater for children and the disabled, so no one need feel left out. There is also a superb licensed restaurant on the premises which serves evening meals on request, along with Sunday lunch from an extensive menu at very affordable prices. Recommended by many of the local bed and breakfast establishments, Chancellor's Tea Rooms offer the visitor a terrific selection of home-made culinary delights whatever the time of day.

The streets of Painswick village contain a number of interesting features, including a set of unusual 19th century 'spectacle' stocks in St Mary's street, the part-Tudor Byfield House with its elegant 18th century façade,

Dennis French's renowned Painswick Woodcrafts in New Street, and the fine half-timbered Post Office dating from 1428 which is said to be the oldest functioning post office in the country. There are also two impressive manor houses in Painswick: Court House, which was built in 1604 for a local cloth merchant, and Castle Godwyn, a small 18th century manor owned by the Milne family which is open to visitors all year round by written appointment only.

Chancellor's Tea Rooms, Kingsley House, Victoria Street, Painswick Tel: 01452 812451

Painswick House is located on the northern edge of the village, and although the interior of this splendid Palladian mansion is not open to the public, its six acre grounds are. Hidden in a broad combe, Painswick's **Rococo Garden** contains some attractive old gardeners' outbuildings and delightful woodland walks. (Open Wednesdays to Sundays and Bank Holiday Mondays, 11am to 5pm between 1 February and mid-December.)

The impressive **Hambutt's Mynd Guest House** is situated in a side road just 200 yards from the main road into Painswick. Originally built in the 1700s as a corn mill driven by a windmill, in 1801 it was converted into the first girls' school in Painswick. In later years it was again converted into a normal dwelling house and today, it is a renowned bed and breakfast establishment run by resident proprietors John and Elizabeth. The three guest bedrooms all have colour TVs and full central heating, along with wonderful panoramic views over the surrounding valley and hills.

Hambutt's Mynd Guest House, Edge Road, Painswick
Tel: 01452 812352

Where better to stay to appreciate this beautiful area than **Castle Lodge**? The home of John and Rosemarie Cooke, this magnificent country manor house is situated in a charming position opposite Poper's Wood and overlooking Painswick Valley, within easy reach of the Cotswolds Way,

Castle Lodge, The Beacon, Painswick Tel: 01452 813603

one of the most famous long distance walks in the UK.

Only a short walk away are spectacular views of the golf course and Painswick Beacon; or why not walk through Poper's Wood to Prinknash Abbey? John and Rosemarie extend a very warm welcome to all their guests and are highly regarded, not only for the comfort of their spacious and luxurious en-suite accommodation, but also for their stupendous English breakfasts! Their wealth of local knowledge is second to none, and many guests have become regulars, returning year after year to sample their unique brand of hospitality.

The upland area to the west of Painswick offers some magnificent views of the Severn Vale and the Forest of Dean. The National Trust-owned **Haresfield Beacon** overlooks the River Severn as it bends around the Arlingham peninsula and is the site of a once strategically important Roman hill fort. A short distance away, the outline of an early British encampment known as **Broadbarrow Green** can also be detected. At 700 feet above sea level, it is possible to see for over 50 miles from the summit on a clear day.

EDGE

The aptly-named village of Edge lies on the fall of the Cotswold escarpment, two miles northeast of Haresfield Beacon. Situated on the main A4173 Stroud to Gloucester road, the **Edgemoor Inn** is a fine old pub which enjoys panoramic views of the surrounding hills.

The Edgemoor Inn, Edge, Near Stroud Tel: 01452 813576

The building is constructed of mellow Cotswold stone which has weathered with age to create a warm inviting glow, even from the outside. Owned and personally run since 1991 by Chris and Jill, the inn is a testimony to their ability for making visitors feel at home. The bar exudes a warm and friendly atmosphere, and the choice of traditional ales is second to none. An excellent range of meals and bar snacks is available at lunchtimes and in the evening, all freshly prepared on the premises and offered at very competitive prices. Outside, there is a pretty patio terrace where customers can enjoy a quiet drink or eat al fresco on those warm summer evenings. There are also good facilities for children and the disabled in this typical and very welcoming country pub. Please note, pets are not allowed.

HARESFIELD

A couple of miles along the base of the Cotswold escarpment to the west, the village of Haresfield is home to the widely renowned **Countryside Centre**. This attractive wildlife garden contains a large walk-through aviary, a pets' and small animals' corner, a series of interesting nature trails, and a superb collection of owls and other birds of prey. A wildlife rescue unit and sanctuary is also based here. (Open daily, 10am to 4.30pm, all year round.)

BROOKTHORPE

The country lanes to the northeast of Haresfield lead to Brookthorpe, a pleasant village containing a 13th century church with an unusual saddleback tower.

GLOUCESTER

From here, the A4173 leads to the centre of Gloucester, a city with a surprising amount to offer the visitor, partly because of its long and distinguished history, and partly because of the revitalisation that has taken place in recent years, particularly around its old docks. Although there was a settlement here during the Iron Age, it was the Roman legions who made an indelible impression on this strategically important site following their invasion of southern England in the 1st century AD. Their first undertaking was to erect a fort to guard what was then the lowest crossing point on the Severn. This was followed about twenty years later by the building of a much larger fortress on higher ground, and within a few years, the new Roman settlement of Glevum had become an important military base which was to play a vital role in confining the rebellious Celts and Britons to the bleak uplands of Wales. The location of the later fortifications can still be seen in the modern street plan at the place now known as Gloucester Cross, where the four streets of Westgate, Northgate, Eastgate and Southgate converge.

A Saxon monastery was founded in Gloucester in the 7th century, and after the Norman invasion, William the Conqueror continued the Saxon tradition of holding a Christmas court here. Indeed, it was in Gloucester in 1085 that he took the decision to commission the Domesday Book. He also ordered the rebuilding of the abbey, a task which took 33 years to complete and included the construction of a magnificent great church, the forerunner of **Gloucester Cathedral**.

Two rows of colossal Norman pillars dominate the Cathedral's 174 foot long nave, the original timber roof of which was replaced in 1242 by stone vaulting in Early English style. The Norman presbytery and choir were replaced in the 14th

century, and the west end of the nave was rebuilt in Perpendicular style during the 15th century. At 72 feet by 38 feet, the great east window is the largest surviving medieval stained-glass window in the country. It was built to celebrate the victory at the Battle of Crécy in 1346 and depicts the coronation of the Virgin surrounded by a colourful entourage of saints, popes and monarchs.

Gloucester Cathedral

The Cathedral contains a number of interesting monuments, most notably the wooden effigy of Robert Duke of Normandy dating from 1134, and the elaborate carved tomb of Edward II, murdered at Berkeley Castle in 1327 by his queen and her lover. Constructed in the 14th century, the exquisite cathedral cloisters contain some of the finest fan tracery still in existence. An excellent view of the 225 foot cathedral tower can be had from the cloisters garden. The cathedral also houses an exhibition of church plate from the Anglican Treasury. (Open Mondays to Saturdays, 10.30am to 4pm, Easter and November; admission free.)

The old nucleus of the city around Gloucester Cross contains some fine early buildings. Among them is the ancient **Church of St Mary de Crypt** in Southgate Street, **St John's Church** in Northgate Street, the home of Robert Raikes, founder of the Sunday School Movement, in Ladybellegate Street, and the 19th century **Guildhall** in Eastgate Street. A good way to explore the city is to join one of the guided walks which leave the tourist information centre at St Michael's Tower at 2.30pm on Wednesdays and Sundays (more frequently in summer). A map of the Via Sacra, a self-guided tour around old Gloucester, is also available here.

During the 14th and 15th centuries, three great inns were established in Gloucester to cater for the pilgrims who came to visit the tomb of Edward II. Two of these remain today: the magnificent galleried New Inn, which was founded by a monk from the abbey in 1450, is situated close to Gloucester Cross in Northgate Street, and the Fleece Hotel, which has a stone-vaulted undercroft dating from the 12th century, can be found in Westgate Street.

Another building worth making the effort to find is **Maverdine House**, an imposing four-storey residence which was occupied by the commander of the Parliamentarian garrison during the Civil War siege of 1643. Despite most of Wessex being in Royalist hands, the strategically-important city of Gloucester held out for Cromwell and survived a month-long siege by an army under the personal command of Charles I. Colonel Massey's headquarters can be reached via a passageway adjacent to No 26 Westgate Street.

Gloucester's **City Museum and Art Gallery** is situated opposite the Gloucestershire College of Art in Brunswick Road, a short distance from the main shopping centre. This handsome honey-coloured building contains a treasure of rare and beautiful artefacts originating from both the city and county of Gloucester. A three ton Roman column in the entrance hall provides a foretaste of the exhibits highlighted in the darkened interior of the archaeology gallery. The superbly-engraved **Birdlip Mirror**, made in bronze for a Celtic chief just before the Roman conquest, is on display here, as are two Roman tombstones, one depicting a horseman spearing a British soldier, and the other a merchant wearing a thick cloak. Perhaps most impressive, however, is the gallery floor which is cut away to reveal the Roman city wall which passes under the building.

Gloucester City Museum and Art Gallery

Other noteworthy exhibits include a Norman backgammon (or tables) set dating from around AD 1100 which is unique in Europe. On the hour, the gallery echoes with the chimes of 18th century grandfather clocks, including a fine Gloucester-made piece which only needs to be wound once a year. A number of English landscape paintings of the 18th and 19th centuries are also on display, including works by Gainsborough, Richard Wilson and Turner, and there is also a natural history gallery containing a beehive, small aquarium, and the massive bones of a 60 foot plesiosaur 'sea-dragon' which were discovered in the north Cotswolds. (Open Mondays to Saturdays, 10am to 5pm, all year round; admission free.)

The 16th century timber-framed house known as **Bishop Hooper's Lodging** can be found in Westgate Street. This is thought to be the place where the martyred Protestant Bishop spent his last night before being burnt at the stake in 1555. Today, the building and its immediate neighbours house one of the most highly regarded folk museums in the country, the **Gloucester Folk Museum**. Here, the social history of Gloucester and its county are brought to life in a series of beautifully laid-out displays. These include a reconstruction of an 18th century pin making factory, a cobbler's workshop, a dairy, and a 19th century schoolroom. Artefacts on show include historic farm implements, tools, kitchen equipment, toys, dolls and a number of relics from the Civil War siege. A series of special exhibitions are held at regular intervals, and to the rear, there is a lovely secluded courtyard with its own herb garden. (Open Mondays to Saturdays, 10am to 5pm, all year round; admission free.)

Situated within 200 yards of the Folk Museum, the **Gloucester Transport Museum** in Bearland houses an interesting small collection of historic vehicles. Exhibits on show include a horse-drawn tram from around 1880, a fire engine from around 1895, and an early 19th century baby carriage. Children of all ages will be interested in the **World of Beatrix Potter** at 9 College Court. The shop is believed to have inspired her much loved story, *The Tailor Of Gloucester*, which is based on a local folk tale. Today, this commercially-run gift shop contains a number of interesting displays relating to the life and work of Beatrix Potter, including a working model of the mice stitching the Mayor of Gloucester's waistcoat.

Throughout its history, Gloucester has been an important river port on the busy route between the Midlands and the Bristol Channel. Queen Elizabeth I granted the city formal port status in 1580, however, the introduction of larger vessels during the 18th century necessitated the building of a canal to link Gloucester with the deep water of the Severn estuary. The canal was finally completed in 1827, resulting in a boom in commercial activity which lasted for several decades.

From the 1860s onwards, however, the area around **Gloucester Docks** suffered a steady decline due to competition from more efficient rail and road transport. By the end of the 1970s, the docks were virtually derelict and a radical solution was needed to secure the area's future.

After much consideration, an ambitious project of renovation was initiated which was to transform the 23 acre site into a vibrant cultural centre which today should be included on every visitor's itinerary. The handsome old warehouse buildings have been converted for use as commercial units and flats, and a stylish new shopping area, Merchants' Quay, has been constructed on the waterfront. A converted barge, the Semington, now operates as an arts centre and café.

There is also a bustling **Antiques Centre** where anything from a small item of bric-a-brac to an expensive piece of antique furniture can be found. The centre is housed in a restored 19th century warehouse which stands in the northeast corner of Gloucester's rejuvenated docklands. One of the widest selections of antiques under one roof, the centre attracts both trade and private collectors with its vast display of furniture, porcelain, jewellery and other collectibles. The building incorporates a licensed restaurant and is open seven days a week.

Gloucester Antiques Centre, Severn Road, Gloucester
Tel: 01452 529716 Fax: 01452 307161

Three floors of the recently converted Llanthony Warehouse are taken up by the **National Waterways Museum**, a fascinating attraction devoted to the 200 year period when Britain's inland waterways carried the goods of the nation.

National Waterways Museum

The building, which itself forms part of the museum, is named after Llanthony Priory, a ruined monastery on the eastern edge of the Welsh

Black Mountains which in its heyday was one of the wealthiest and most influential in the country.

The exhibits include working engines and models, live craft demonstrations, archive film presentations, and hands-on computer simulations of canal navigation. A number of barges and narrowboats are moored outside on the quayside, one of which, the Queen Boadicea II, takes visitors on short cruises around the docklands area. The site also encompasses a working forge, a massive 'No 4' steam dredger, a shire horse stable, and a number of canal-related workshops. (Open daily, 10am to 6pm (5pm in winter), all year round.)

Gloucester's **Victoria Dock** is now a thriving marina. Here, the Albert Warehouse, an impressive converted storehouse, is the location of another specialist museum, Robert Opie's **Museum of Advertising and Packaging**. Robert Opie is an enthusiastic collector of commercial ephemera who has assembled around 30,000 items of packaging and advertising over the last 20 years. The result is a fascinating exhibition which offers a real insight into the presentation of consumer products since the mid-1800s. Along with items of consumer packaging, the museum contains an interesting collection of posters, enamel signs and point-of-sale promotions which together chronicle the changing trends in popular taste. There is also a continuous presentation of vintage television commercials. (Open daily, 10am to 6pm, all year round; closed Mondays in winter.)

Gloucester's old Custom House is the home of the recently-modernised **Regiments of Gloucestershire Museum**, winner of the prestigious Museum of the Year Award in 1991 for best small museum. This absorbing exhibition gives an animated account of the county's two army regiments, the 'Glorious Glosters' and the Royal Gloucestershire Hussars, over their distinguished 300 year history. (Open Tuesdays to Sundays, 10am to 5pm, all year round.)

TWIGWORTH

From the centre of Gloucester, it is worth making a short detour north along the A38 Tewkesbury road to visit Twigworth, home of the internationally renowned museum of wildlife art. **Nature In Art** is housed in a fine Georgian mansion, Wallsworth Hall, which dates from the 1740s and is set in its own grounds three miles from the city centre.

(Open Tuesdays to Sundays (and Bank Holiday Mondays), 10am to 5pm, all year round.)

OVER

Crossing to the western side of the Severn, **Over Farm** at Over grows over 70 vegetable and fruit crops during the year, including strawberries and raspberries in summer. Along with an impressive farm market, the farm boasts some unusual farm animals, including African ostriches and water buffalo. (Open daily, all year round.)

ASHLEWORTH

A few miles further north, turn east off the A417 at Hartpury to reach the delightful riverside settlement of Ashleworth. The focal point of the village is the 12th century **Church of St Andrew and Bartholomew** which has some unusual herringbone masonry and a 14th century spire. The church is surrounded by attractive medieval buildings, including a magnificent 15th century **Tithe Barn** which has two projecting stone porches and an elaborate system of interlocking roof timbers with queenposts. The barn is owned by the National Trust and is open daily, 9am to 6pm between April and the end of October.

The surrounding estate once belonged to the abbey of St Augustine in Bristol. It contains two splendid 15th century manor houses: the handsome stone-built **Ashleworth Court** and the timber-framed **Ashleworth Manor**. The latter was originally built as the abbot's summer residence and has since been enlarged. (Both are open to the public by written arrangement only; for information, telephone 01452 70241 and 70350 respectively.) The village pub, the Boat Inn, has been in the hands of the Jelf family for over a hundred years. During the English Civil War, one of their ancestors is said to have ferried Charles I across the Severn and as a reward, he was granted a monopoly to convey passengers at this point. Foscombe, an elaborate 19th century Gothic mansion standing on a low hill overlooking the river, was once owned by the Rolling Stones' drummer, Charlie Watts.

TIRLEY

Situated at Tirley, in the lanes three miles to the northeast of Ashleworth, **Town Street Farm** is a typical working family farm which offers excellent bed and breakfast accommodation. The farmhouse is appointed to an exceptionally high standard and offers two spacious, centrally heated guest rooms with colour TV, tea/coffee making facilities, and an en-suite toilet and shower complete with soap and towels. A farmhouse breakfast is served each morning in the sun room, overlooking the garden with its lawns and flower beds. The food is varied and delicious, and guaranteed to satisfy until lunchtime and beyond.

Owned and personally run by Sue Warner, Town Street Farm offers a relaxing country break complete with hill-walking over the Malverns, or simply sitting by the river sampling the local brews. On the farm there are dogs, chickens, horses and ponies, and riding can be arranged at certain times of the year, as can tennis on Sue's own tennis court, though soft-soled shoes are essential. Ideally situated overlooking hills and meadows, though still within easy reach of the M5 and M50, Town Street Farm provides an ideal year-round base for exploring this delightful part of the Severn valley.

Town Street Farm, Tirley, Near Tewkesbury Tel: 01452 780442

SNIG'S END

The charmingly named village of Snig's End lies a little further north along the A417. At the centre of the settlement is a crescent of sturdy yet attractive stone cottages which date from the time the village formed the nucleus of a Chartist land colony. Founded in 1847 by Feargus

O'Connor, the colony placed great importance on education, building a substantial school to serve the few dozen resident families who formed the community of self-supporting smallholdings. Sadly though, the project failed within six years thanks to a combination of inadequate financing, confused aims, poor soil, inaccessible markets and a population of townspeople ill-suited to rural life. All that remains of the Chartist Utopia is the crescent of well-built cottages and the old schoolhouse, now the Prince of Wales Inn.

STAUNTON

A couple of miles northwest of Staunton, the A417 passes to the east of **Pauntley Court**, a private country residence which was built on the site of a medieval manor house. In the 14th century, this was the birthplace of Dick Whittington, the pantomime hero who in reality became Lord Mayor of London on three occasions between 1397 and 1419. Whittington was no poor boy who made his fortune with the assistance of a quick-witted cat; he was the offspring of a wealthy landed family who went on to grow even wealthier as a mercer in the City of London. (The only other fact that consistent with the pantomime story was that he married Alice Fitzwarren, the daughter of a wealthy Dorset knight.)

Why the famous pantomime legend grew up around Sir Richard Whittington of Pauntley is unknown, although similar rags-to-riches stories are said to exist in countries all over the world. One event which contributed to the myth was the discovery of a carving in the foundations of a medieval house in Gloucester in 1862. A depiction of a youth holding some kind of animal, it became widely known as 'Dick and his Cat' and was responsible for establishing the legend in the British Isles. Today, the carving can be seen in Gloucester's Folk Museum.

DYMOCK

Four miles further west, the village of Dymock is a delightful collection of cottages loosely arranged around the early-Norman **Church of St Mary**. Set beside the pleasantly shaded Wintour's Green, the church contains some unusual artefacts, including Dymock's last railway ticket issued in September 1959. The older buildings of northwest Gloucestershire differ from those in the east of county in that they are often built of red brick instead of Cotswold stone. Dymock contains some fine examples of early brick building, including the White House and the Old Rectory near the church, and the Old Grange which lies three-quarters-of-a-mile to the northwest and incorporates the remains of the Cistercian abbey of Flaxley.

In the years immediately prior to World War I, a group of writers based in the area became known as the Dymock Poets. The group, which included Rupert Brooke, sent their quarterly poetry magazine *New Numbers* to addresses throughout the world from Dymock's tiny post office, causing the village to become something of a literary mecca.

KEMPLEY

A couple of miles west of Dymock, Kempley's **Church of St Mary** is an early-Norman gem which was built between 1090 and 1100 in a position to the south of the present day village. Inside, the chancel contains a virtually complete set of 12th century frescoes, the most acclaimed examples of their kind in the region. It is believed these exquisite paintings were created to assist the local priest in conveying the rudiments of the scriptures to his uneducated flock. A series of 14th century tempera paintings can also be found in the nave. Both sets of frescoes were concealed behind several coats of whitewash in the mid-16th century where they remained undiscovered until 1872. A major renovation carried out in the 1950s then restored them to their former glory.

The village of Kempley contains another interesting building, the red sandstone **Church of St Edward the Confessor**, which was constructed in 1903 according to the highest traditions of the Arts and Crafts Movement. Most of the fabric was made by local craftspeople using readily-available materials, including the imposing scissor beams which were fashioned from green oak taken from the nearby Beauchamp estate.

NEWENT

From Kempley, a minor road leads southeast across the M50 to the old market town of Newent, the capital of the area of northwest Gloucestershire known as the **Ryelands**. The route into the town from the north passes the Three Choirs Vineyard, a working vineyard producing good quality English wines which visitors are invited to sample and buy. (Open daily, 9am to 5pm, all year round.)

Newent stands at the centre of the broad triangle of land known as 'Daffodil Crescent' where in spring, a delicate small flower known as the

Lent lily grows prolifically in the wild. The rich, brightly-coloured soil of the Leadon Valley was traditionally used for growing rye and raising Ryeland sheep, an ancient breed which produced wool of such quality that it sold for twice the price of its Cotswold equivalent. Between the 16th and 18th centuries, the town grew to become one of Gloucestershire's principal wool-trading centres, a factor accounting for the large number of period merchants' houses that can be seen here today.

The nave of Newent's medieval **Church** had to be completely rebuilt after Royalist troops removed the lead from its roof to make bullets, an act which caused it to collapse during a heavy snowfall in 1674. Construction of the new nave only went ahead after Charles II agreed to donate 60 tons of timber from the Forest of Dean. Newent's most distinctive building, however, can be found on the old Market Square - the splendid timber-framed **Market House**. Originally constructed as a butter market in 1668, its upper floors are supported on sixteen oak pillars which form a unique open colonnade.

Old Court Hotel, Church Street, Newent Tel: 01531 820522

The elegant **Old Court Hotel** stands in beautiful grounds surrounded by lawns and trees, with a curving gravel driveway leading up to its impressive entrance. Once the home of the lord of the manor, Old Court stands on the site of an ancient Benedictine priory. The owners, Sue and Ron Wood, have carefully modernised the building whilst retaining many of its original period features, including the magnificent plasterwork ceiling in the Green Drawing Room. The Court Restaurant, with its Georgian panelled walls, is spacious and welcoming. The cuisine has been carefully developed over the years, and now combines the finest English tastes with a more flamboyant French influence. The six guest bedrooms are individually styled and include private facilities, hospitality tray, radio, TV, and of course, warmth and comfort. Situated adjacent to the church in Newent, the Old Court Hotel is English Tourist Board 3 crowns commended.

Those interested in finding out more about Newent's past should make a point of visiting **The Shambles Museum of Victorian Life** in Church Street. This impressive museum is laid out as a Victorian town complete with cobbled streets, gas-fired lamps, shops and workrooms. The core of the museum is a four-storey house which has been furnished throughout as a Victorian draper's home. (The name 'shambles', however, comes from the Old English word for slaughterhouse, indicating the building once belonged to a butcher.) To the rear, the narrow alleyways contain over 30 shops and workshops, including a chemist, dairy, pawnbroker, ironmonger and blacksmith. There is also a modern gift shop and tearoom. (Open Tuesdays to Sundays and Bank Holiday Mondays, 10am to 6pm between 1 March and 31 October, plus weekends only until Christmas.)

The tradition of glass making was established in Newent by French Huguenot refugees in the 17th century. This highly-skilled practice has been revived in recent years at the Glassbarn in Culver Street. Here, visitors can see the intricate process of glass-blowing and view the items of finished glassware in the gallery. (Open Mondays to Fridays, 10am to 5pm, all year round)

Another of Newent's attractions is the Butterfly Centre in Birches Lane, just to the north of the town centre. As well as being able to see exotic butterflies flying freely in the tropical house, visitors can tour the menagerie, aquarium, natural history exhibition and garden centre. (Open daily, 10am to 5pm between Easter and October.)

Newent's famous **National Bird of Prey Centre** can be found on the western side of the B4216, one mile south of the town. The centre boasts the largest private collection of birds of prey in Europe, including eagles, hawks, falcons, owls, condors and vultures. The site incorporates a number of aviaries which have been set aside for breeding purposes, as well as the renowned Falconry Centre where visitors can have the exhilarating experience of observing trained birds in free flight. Weather permitting, up to four flying demonstrations are offered each day. (Open daily, 10.30am to 5.30pm between February and November.)

TAYNTON

A couple of miles further south, Taynton is an attractive hamlet which in springtime is filled with daffodils. The village church is unusual in that it was constructed during Oliver Cromwell's Commonwealth Government. It was the view of the Puritans that the presence of God had no geographical limitations, so it was built along a north-south axis rather than the conventional east-west one. Nearby, Taynton House has three impressive barns, one of which dates from 1695. The **Taynton Farm Centre** in Hown Hall is a working farm which gives visitors the opportunity to meet and learn about the animals. (Open daily, 10am to 6pm between Easter and end-September.)

Two miles west of Taynton, the National Trust-owned **May Hill** is a dramatic and mystical place which is crowned by an unusual copse of trees planted in 1887 to mark Queen Victoria's golden jubilee. This was once the scene of the annual May Games, where the children of the area would meet in mock battle to celebrate the coming of summer. Present-day walkers taking the pleasant stroll to the 969 foot summit are rewarded with magnificent views of the Forest of Dean and the Severn's dramatic horseshoe bend around the Arlingham peninsula.

CHAPTER FIVE
Central Cotswolds

Chastleton Manor, Moreton-in-Marsh

Cirencester

5
Central Cotswolds

CIRENCESTER

Often referred to as the capital of the Cotswolds, the ancient market town of Cirencester has a history dating back to the Roman occupation of Britain. In AD 47, the Romans built the Fosse Way, one of four major roads in Britain, to link the prosperous wool-based centres of southwest England with Lincoln and the military garrisons of the north. A series of defensive fortifications were constructed along its length, including one which was sited at the junction with Ermin Street and Akeman Street, two other Roman highways. This fort quickly grew to become Corinium Dobunnorum, the second most important Roman settlement in Britain after Londinium. It was named after a conquered tribe, the Dobunni, who inhabited much of the South West.

Little evidence of Cirencester's Roman roots can be seen in situ today. However, the award-winning **Corinium Museum** in Park Street houses one of the finest collections of ancient Roman antiquities in the country. Exhibits include superb sculptures, domestic items and two remarkable floor mosaics: the four seasons and the hunting dogs. There is also a life-size reconstruction of a Roman garden, dining room and kitchen, as well as a cut-away section of a surprisingly sophisticated central-heating system. The Corinium Museum covers the history of locality from prehistoric to medieval times and is open Mondays to Saturdays, 10am to 5.30pm, and Sundays 2pm to 5.30pm, all year round (closed Mondays during winter months).

After a prolonged period of decline which lasted until the Norman Invasion, Cirencester eventually came under the influence of William

Corinium Museum, Cirencester

FitzOrbern, the Earl of Hereford. In 1117, King Henry I founded the Augustinian Abbey of St Mary here which survived until Henry VIII's Dissolution of the Monasteries in the mid-16th century. Little of this now remains except for a single Norman arch which can be seen in the northeastern corner of the Abbey Grounds. The grounds now form an attractive park containing a lake, trees and a lively population of wildfowl. An outline of the original abbey walls can also be seen here, along with the only surviving section of the old Roman fortifications.

Cirencester's church of St John the Baptist was built in the 15th and 16th centuries and is perhaps the finest example of a Cotswold 'wool' church. Like many other churches in the area, its construction was financed by the wealthy wool merchants who prospered during that period. (Such churches can often be identified by the fact they were built to a grander scale than befits the size of the community they now serve.) The funds for the pinnacled tower, however, came from a different source - the Earls of Salisbury and Kent. They rebelled against Henry IV and were arrested by the people of Cirencester as they passed through the town in 1399. After executing the rebellious pair, King Henry allowed the townsfolk to keep the contents of the earls' strongboxes, a sum which covered the cost of building the church tower.

St John's Church is built of golden Cotswold stone and stands in a magnificent position in the Market Place. Its pulpit is shaped like an enormous wineglass, and the 17th century hourglass which stands close by was once used to keep a check on the duration of the preacher's sermons. A statue of a blue-coated boy stands beside the door to the south aisle. This was used in the 18th century to collect funds for the church primary school which was founded in 1714 and still flourishes today.

The famous silver and gilt Boleyn Cup can also be found in the south aisle. This was made for Henry VIII's second wife in 1535, the year before she was executed for alleged adultery. Anne's personal insignia - a rose tree and a falcon holding a sceptre - can be seen on the lid. Look out also for the depiction of a cat chasing a mouse, a medieval craftsmen's joke which can be seen in the Lady Chapel.

Although no longer open at set hours, parties can arrange to climb the 120 foot West Tower by contacting the vicar. Visitors ascend past a peal of twelve church bells made by Rudhall of Gloucester which are believed to be the earliest of their kind in the country. Those making it to the top are rewarded with a breathtaking bird's eye view of Cirencester's ancient network of streets. Clearly identifiable are Spitalgate, with its 12th century remains of the Hospital of St John, and Coxwell Street with its fine row of original wool-merchants' houses and artisans' cottages. It is also possible to see over the 40 foot yew hedge which was planted in 1818 to conceal **Cirencester House**, the home of the Earl Bathurst, from prying eyes.

Cirencester also contains a number of impressive visitor attractions. **Brewery Arts** in Brewery Court is a living craft centre where resident craftspeople can be seen making jewellery, baskets and other hand-made crafts. The building also contains an attractive coffee house, craft shop and exhibition space. (Open daily, all year round.) The **Corn Hall** in the Market Place hosts a popular antiques market on Fridays and a craft market on Saturdays, along with a variety of other events, including sales of linen and books.

Cirencester House stands at the top of Cecily Hill on the western edge of town and although not open to the public, its grounds are. Walkers and horse riders are permitted to roam freely over the 3000 acre **Cirencester Park** which has pathways stretching almost as far as Sapperton, five miles to the west. The park was laid out in the 18th century by the First Earl Bathurst with the assistance of his friend, Alexander Pope. Pope's

Seat, an elegant summerhouse standing at the point where ten pathways meet, was one of the poet's favourite places of contemplation.

Set in beautiful surroundings next to Cirencester Park, the **Cirencester Open Air Swimming Pool** is one of the oldest outdoor pools in the country. Built in 1869, both the main and paddling pools are supplied with natural water from a private well. (Open daily between May and mid-September.) An impressively-equipped all year round leisure facility is available at the **Cotswold Leisure Centre** in Tetbury Road.

The remains of the **Bull Ring**, a once glorious Roman amphitheatre which is perhaps the largest and best preserved example of its kind in Britain, can be found on a site to the west of Cirencester. Best approached from Querns Hill and Cotswold Avenue, the remains consist of an oval arena with twin entrances and a series of sloping earth banks which would have supported rows of timber seating. The **Chesterton Farm Shop**, a working farm offering organic meats and fresh fruit and vegetables, can be found off Chesterton Lane in the southwestern outskirts of the town.

DAGLINGWORTH

To the northwest of Cirencester, a series of five delightful settlements are sited along the exquisite valley of the River Dunt, or Duntbrook. Just to the east, the A417 diverts the speeding traffic along the undeviating course of the former Roman highway, Ermin Street. However, this charming little valley gives the impression of lying a million miles from the pressures of modern civilisation.

The church in Daglingworth contains a number of wonderfully preserved Anglo-Saxon sculptures which are renowned for their simple artistry. The village also has a handsome, if somewhat exposed, Georgian house, a large Victorian former rectory, and a number of characteristic Cotswold cottages belonging to the Duchy of Cornwall.

DUNTISBOURNE ROUSE

Further upstream, the road next passes through Duntisbourne Rouse. This also possesses a fine church, the tiny **St Michael's**, which has some fine features dating back to Saxon and Norman times. The 15th century west tower has a rare saddleback roof and, inside, there is a wonderful Norman crypt and font.

DUNTISBOURNE ABBOTS

The road fords Duntbrook in both **Middle Duntisbourne** and **Duntisbourne Leer**. The latter of these two tranquil hamlets once belonged to the abbey of Lire in France. In Duntisbourne Abbots at the northern end of the valley, the old cobbled road actually follows the course of the stream as it flows through the village between two raised walls. In the days of horse-drawn transport, carters would come here to clean their wagons and wash their horses hooves in the flowing water. Despite the risk of flooding, the present inhabitants continue to resist any plan to divert the course of the river. It is also worth having a look at the mossy stone pool which once supplied the community with its water.

SAPPERTON

The attractive village of Sapperton lies in the lanes to the southwest of the Duntisbournes, just north of the main A419 Cirencester to Stroud road. Here, the Thames-Severn Canal emerges from the remarkable two mile long **Sapperton Tunnel** which, on its completion in 1798, was the longest in England's canal system. Closed in 1911, the tunnel has a Gothic western portal at Daneway, and a classical eastern portal at Coates, the latter having been restored as part of an ambitious plan to reopen the entire waterway.

There are also interesting pubs at either end: the 18th century Daneway Inn to the west, and the Tunnel House at Coates to the east. These were once the haunts of bargees and professional 'leggers', freelance artisans who used to 'walk' the narrowboats through the tunnel by lying on their backs and pushing against the walls and roof with their legs.

The village of Sapperton contains a number of fine old buildings, some dating from the 17th century and others built in sympathetic style during an Edwardian revival which came to an end with the outbreak of World War I. It was during this period that Ernest and Sidney Barnsley and Ernest Gimson founded a group of local artist-craftspeople known as the Sapperton Group. This had close links with the followers of William Morris and was centred around nearby **Daneway House**, an elegant manor house dating from the 14th and 17th centuries. The group's furniture workshops and showrooms were based here, and these can still be viewed by appointment only at any reasonable time between March and October. The founders of the group also designed and built a number of distinctive houses for themselves in the village.

FRAMPTON MANSELL

A mile-and-a-half further west, Frampton Mansell is a pleasant village containing some photogenic old buildings, including a manor farm which was built in the time of Charles II, and the village church which dates from a more recent period than its Norman appearance would suggest.

Crown Hotel and Restaurant, Frampton Mansell
Tel: 01285 760601 Fax: 01285 760681

Situated just five miles from Stroud, the **Crown Hotel and Restaurant** at Frampton Mansell is one of those really special places which is worth stepping a little way off the beaten track to find. This impressive establishment offers the very finest hospitality, and with the help of charming host Julia Corin-Richards AHCIMA, visitors are immediately made to feel at home in these warm and friendly surroundings. As well as providing a superb range of food and drink, the Crown offers comfortable accommodation in twelve en-suite guest rooms, each with colour television, direct-dial telephone and tea/coffee making facilities. In the morning, guests are offered the choice of either a continental or full English breakfast. The immediate area is so well provided with picturesque villages, country inns and attractive walks that the car becomes almost redundant during the time spent in this beautiful part of the country.

Frampton Mansell also has something really out of the ordinary to offer those seeking self-catering accommodation with a difference. **Twissells Mill** is an English Tourist Board 4 key approved establishment which is situated in a converted 18th century mill. Proprietors Daphne and Martin

Neville live next door in Baker's Mill, a property which has been used as a location for several films, including BBC TV's *House of Elliot*. Set in a truly wonderful position in the **Golden Valley**, the grounds at the back of the mill incorporate a two-and-a-half acre lake on which guests may boat. If that is not enough, there is also Mr Bee and Little Bee, the TV otters! This delightful pair live beside the River Frome where they lead a carefree semi-wild life. Visitors may get an insight into the antics of these charming television personalities as they somersault in their own swimming pool, or emerge from their cosy hay-filled hutch. The immediate area abounds with birdlife and wild badgers, and offers endless opportunities for country walks. The Nevilles have three boisterous dogs who enjoy taking their guests for a stroll, and the local pubs offer good food and drink at modest cost. As well as offering a superb holiday base, this wonderful hideaway offers a luxury quality of life!

Twissells Mill, Frampton Mansell Tel: 01285 760234

CHALFORD

The picturesque community of Chalford is spread over the steep northern slope of the Golden Valley in a maze of narrow lanes. Lying just three miles to the southeast of Stroud, this is the centre of the area known as the

'Alpine Cotswolds', and at one time food and fuel had to be delivered up the steep gradient by donkey. Today, Chalford is best explored on foot, its tight thoroughfares being filled with interesting shops and pubs. Though not impressive architecturally, the **Church** contains some interesting pieces of furniture made by craftsmen Peter Van Der Waals, Norman Jewson and WG Simmonds. The Round House, an unusual example of a former canal lengthman's house, stands opposite.

Visitors looking for bed and breakfast accommodation in a fine period house in the heart of the beautiful Golden Valley should look no further than **Green Court**. Located on the edge of Chalford on the way in from Frampton Mansell, this delightful establishment has three comfortable and spacious guest rooms, each with superb countryside views and all the usual facilities. Jan Bateman is a very friendly and capable hostess who serves a superb breakfast which is guaranteed to prepare her guests for a busy day exploring the local villages and countryside. Children and pets are very welcome, as are the disabled, though prior notice is appreciated so that everything can be made ready for their arrival. With its extremely relaxed and welcoming atmosphere, guests will wish to return to this charming establishment again and again.

Green Court, The High Street, Chalford Tel: 01453 883234

BOURNES GREEN

A pleasant walk from Chalford leads to the isolated hamlets of **France Lynch**, **Avenis Green** and Bournes Green, where there is an imposing Victorian parish Church dating from 1856 and a disused 17th century

Congregational Church whose decaying churchyard contains the graves of several old Puritan families.

Conveniently situated off the A419 midway between Cirencester and Stroud, **Westley Farm** provides outstanding self-catering accommodation in the heart of the southern Cotswolds. Its once redundant stone outbuildings have been tastefully converted to provide four impressive holiday cottages and two flats, each sleeping from two to five people. All are superbly equipped with night storage heating, washing machines, telephones, televisions and open log fires, and there is also a farm shop. Set on the steep slopes of the beautiful Golden Valley with breathtaking views all around, this 80 acre working farm raises cattle, sheep, horses and domestic fowl. Excellent horse riding and pony trekking facilities lie within two miles, and the surrounding countryside is crisscrossed with numerous well-maintained woodland paths and bridleways. Whether on foot, in the car or on horseback, Westley Farm provides an ideal holiday base for touring the beautiful Cotswold countryside.

Westley Farm, Near Chalford Tel: 01285 760262

OAKRIDGE LYNCH

Overlooking the Golden Valley in the very heart of the Gloucestershire countryside, the **Butchers Arms** is a gem of a village pub which is owned and personally-run by Brian and Peter Coupe. Located at Oakridge Lynch in the hills to the northeast of Chalford, this lively Cotswold inn is packed with genuine atmosphere, with traditional furnishings and open fires in colder weather. Renowned for its food, visitors come from miles around to enjoy a lunchtime meal or snack in the bar. The Stable Room is open for evening meals from 7.30pm on Wednesdays to Saturdays, and a traditional lunch is served from 12 noon on Sundays. Table reservations are recommended as the inn proves very popular at meal times. There is also a fine selection of up to six real ales, all kept in perfect condition, as well as the usual spirits, lager, cider and wines from around the world. The Butchers Arms also has a large beer garden which is ideal for children and pets. Everyone finds a welcome at this superb free house!

Butchers Arms, Oakridge Lynch Tel No: 01285 760371

BISLEY

The country lanes to the northwest of Oakridge Lynch lead across rolling Cotswold countryside to the atmospheric village of Bisley. This historic settlement which stands 780 feet above sea level is known by local people as 'Bisley-God-Help-Us' because of the winter winds which sweep across the exposed hillside. The gabled Cotswold houses stand huddled together against the hillside which appears to form a semicircular amphitheatre when approached from the southwest.

Once an important wool centre, in its time the village has also been known as 'Beggarly Bisley' because of the hardship the inhabitants suffered during the decline in the textile industry leading Butchers Arms, Oakridge Lynch Tel: 01285 760371up to the Industrial Revolution. The upper storey of the 17th century **Bear Inn** at the top of George Street is supported by a striking stone colonnade, and nearby there is an unusual little building which once functioned as the village lockup.

Bisley's impressive **All Saints' Church** dates from the 13th century and was restored during the early 19th century by Thomas Keble, the brother of poet and theologian John Keble after whom Keble College, Oxford was named. Thomas Keble was responsible for restoring the seven wells of Bisley which are set in an arc below the Church. In 1863, he also founded the annual custom of 'dressing the wells' on Ascension Day, an event which continues to be witnessed by hundreds of spectators to this day. A decaying ornamental construction in the churchyard known as the 'Poor Souls' Light' dates from the 13th century and was used to hold candles lit for the souls languishing in purgatory. It is thought to be the only outdoor structure of its type in the country.

Perhaps the village's main claim to fame however, is the legend of the 'Bisley Boy'. In the days of its wool-based prosperity, Bisley possessed a royal manor, Over Court, where the young Princess Elizabeth (who went on to become Queen Elizabeth I) stayed on a number of occasions. Rumour has it that during one of these visits, the ten year old princess caught a fever and, to the horror of her hosts, actually died. Fearing the wrath of her father Henry VIII, they hurriedly looked for a substitute and were fortunate enough to find a local child with red hair and remarkably similar physical characteristics. Similar, that is, except for one thing. Elizabeth's stand-in was a local lad called John Neville. Perhaps this would explain the Virgin Queen's reluctance to marry, her problem with hair loss and her 'heart that beats like a man's'?

SLAD

To the west of Bisley, the beautiful Cotswold valley containing the long sprawling village of SLAD was immortalised by Laurie Lee in his autobiographical novel, *Cider With Rosie*. Located just off the A46 Stroud to Cheltenham road, **Upper Vatch Mill** is a superb self-catering cottage set in the very heart of the Cotswold countryside. Owned since 1990 by Ian Hoy, the property is spotlessly clean and excellently equipped with everything a family could need for an enjoyable and trouble-free holiday. Here, guests can step away from the hustle and bustle of everyday life and relax in the tranquil surroundings, then after soaking up the local hospitality and stunning scenery, they can return home with a renewed sense of vitality.

Upper Vatch Mill, The Vatch, Slad Tel: 01453 764270

MISERDEN

From Slad, the minor country roads lead northeastwards to the village of Miserden, home of the renowned **Miserden Park Gardens**. The large sycamore tree marking the centre of this characteristic Cotswold village stands near a 17th century barn which still contains a working forge. Known for their spectacular spring bulbs, roses and topiary, the gardens are situated on the northern side of the village. (Open 10am to 4.30pm, Wednesdays and Thursdays between 1 April and 30 September.)

WHITEWAY

The windswept community of Whiteway is set high on the Cotswold ridge, a mile-and-a-half to the northwest of Miserden. At first sight, the rather inhospitable buildings at the centre of the village give the impression of being home-made. Indeed, many of them were constructed by their owners, a group of Tolstoyan anarchists, who founded the settlement in 1898 following their resettlement from Surrey.

The inhabitants of Whiteway established an economy based on horticulture and cottage industries and at first spurned all interference from the outside world, including police, post office and public transport, in their pursuit of self-sufficiency. This raised a few eyebrows amongst the surrounding population and rumours spread about their suspect moral code, which was said to include open nudity and partner-swapping.

However, unlike many similar Utopian communities, the wooden shacks of Whiteway, along with many of the principles they were founded upon, remain to this day, albeit in a much developed form. A century after it was founded, this unusual village, with its winding lanes, tall hedges and unconventional architecture, is still the domain of creative, liberal-minded individuals.

SEVEN SPRINGS

Four miles northeast of Whiteway, and just to the south of the A436, Seven Springs near Coberley is one of several sites claiming to be the source of the River Thames. Despite the existence of an inscribed stone marker to support this claim, a spring eleven miles to the south at **Thameshead** seems a more likely contender. (This can be found by following a path across some fields behind the Thameshead Inn, a pub on the A433, three miles southwest of Cirencester.) However, Seven Springs remains the undisputed source of the River Churn.

NORTH CERNEY

The A435 to the south of Seven Springs leads to the village of North Cerney, site of one of the most attractive and unusually decorated churches in the Cotswolds. The internal and external walls of this fine 12th century **Church** are etched with extraordinary carved graffiti which is thought to be the work of Tudor masons. Most striking are the representations of mythological animals from the Books of Beasts, or *Bestiaries*, medieval manuscripts renowned for their descriptions of real and mythical animals, many of which have a wider moral significance. The west wall of the Church is scored with a strange long-tailed leopard, and the outer south wall features a congregation-eating manticore (half man, half lion) with three rows of teeth. Grotesque faces look down from the roof-bosses and corbels, and four peer out from the Norman tympanum above the south doorway.

North Cerney is also the location of **Cerney House Gardens**, a romantic secret garden set on a beautiful old country estate. Seasonal attractions include spring bulbs, old-fashioned roses, herbaceous borders, a wild flower bank, tree trail, and kitchen and herb gardens. Selected plants are offered for sale, along with home-produced Cerney Cheese. (Open between April and September.)

BARNSLEY

Four miles southeast of North Cerney, and only three miles from Cirencester along the B4425 Bibury road, the attractive Gloucestershire village of Barnsley is a conservation area which until a few years ago was owned by a single family. Almost all the buildings here are constructed of the same golden limestone, creating a delightful unified character. At one time, all the houses in the village were occupied by local farm workers. Today, however, the estate is owned by a charitable trust which seems willing to sell off vacant properties to outsiders.

Barnsley also has a good pub, an interesting village hall, and a church with an Elizabethan tower. The former rectory, **Barnsley House**, has a renowned garden which contains two elegant 18th century summerhouses, one classical and the other Gothic. (Garden open most Wednesdays.) **Barnsley Park** on the outskirts of the village is a baroque Georgian mansion which is thought to have been designed by Hawksmoor. (Open to visitors by prior appointment only.)

AMPNEY CRUCIS

The three small villages to the south of Barnsley are collectively known as the Ampneys. Lying either side of the A417 on the eastern side of Cirencester, they take their name from Ampney Brook. Furthest upstream is Ampney Crucis, a pleasant community with a large mansion, **Ampney Park**, an old mill, an attractive vicarage and a part-Saxon church which has some interesting medieval paintings and an unusual carved stone cross in its churchyard.

AMPNEY ST MARY

The village of Ampney St Mary was relocated to its present position following the Black Death in the 1300s. All that remains of the original medieval settlement is its 12th century **Church** which stands on its own in the middle of a field half a mile away.

AMPNEY ST PETER

This is perhaps the most attractive of the three villages. It has a small green, a Saxon **Church** with a gabled tower and some noteworthy buildings, including a large house designed by the architect Sidney Gambier-Parry in the 1900s.

SOUTH CERNEY

To the south of Cirencester, the gentle dip slope of the Cotswolds creates an open landscape with river valleys so wide they seem like gentle undulations on a rolling plain. These uppermost reaches of the Thames valley are rich in valuable sand and gravel deposits which have been exploited by the building industry since the 1920s. The sustained removal of the material has left a series of hollows which have gradually filled with water to form a series of shallow freshwater lakes.

These now form an important leisure resource, the **Cotswold Water Park**, which covers a total area of some 22 square miles and contains over 100 man-made lakes. As well as being an important centre for watersports, fishing and general recreational pursuits, it is also an internationally recognised nature conservation area. A large number of waterfowl breed and over-winter here, and several of the lakes and water meadows are designated Sites of Special Scientific Interest.

The park lies to the west of the A419 Cirencester to Swindon road and is spread around the villages of South Cerney and Cerney Wick. Though not a particularly pretty village, South Cerney contains some pleasant old manor houses, a street named Bow Wow, and a church with a carved Norman doorway which contains a rare wooden carving of Christ's head and foot taken from a crucifix in Compostella. There is also a welcoming open farm, **Butts Farm**, stocked with a wide variety of domestic animals and birds. Baby animals can be seen throughout the year, and there is also a children's play area, a pet's corner and a picnic area. (Open Wednesdays to Sundays, 11am to 5pm between Easter and end-September.)

SOMERFORD KEYNES

A couple of miles further west, the Somerford Lakes Reserve near Somerford Keynes offers guided launch trips around a 100 acre lake, taking in an eel and trout farm and a variety of pens containing such exotic fauna as wallabies and ornamental pheasants. (Open all year round to pre-booked parties of four or more.)

DOWN AMPNEY

Situated to the east of the A419 and the Cotswold Water Park, the attractive village of Down Ampney is the birthplace of composer Ralph Vaughan Williams (1872-1958). His music to the hymn *Come Down O*

Fairford

Love Divine is also known as *Down Ampney* after the village of his birth. **All Saints' Church**, where Vaughan Williams' father was incumbent, dates from 1265 and can be seen from miles away across the flat surrounding farmland. The interior is full of atmosphere and contains an interesting reclining effigy of the medieval knight, Sir Nicholas de Valers (or Villiers), in the south transept.

During the Second World War, Down Ampney was the site of an important military airfield and some years after, a stained-glass window was installed in the church in memory of the airmen based here. Each year in September, a service is held to commemorate those lost in the abortive Battle of Arnhem. Not far from the Church, a high yew hedge hides **Down Ampney House**, a handsome Tudor mansion which was partially rebuilt in 1799.

KEMPSFORD

Five miles further east, the network of country lanes leads to Kempsford, a Gloucestershire village with strong Lancastrian connections. The interior of the **Church** is decorated with Lancastrian roses, and the tower is said to have been commissioned by Blanche, wife of John of Gaunt, who was an heir to the first Duke of Lancaster and mother of Henry IV. The horseshoe on the Church door is rumoured to have been shed by the Duke of Lancaster's horse, an incident which had tragic consequences. The byways of Kempsford are haunted by a colourful variety of ghosts, including a silent monk, a youth in lace and breeches, a distraught mother and a repenting knight.

FAIRFORD

This large and bustling village lies on the gently-flowing River Coln, three miles north of Kempsford. This former staging post on the old coaching route between Cirencester and Reading contains a number of buildings of architectural merit.

The **Church of St Mary the Blessed Virgin** contains a truly outstanding set of 15th century stained-glass windows which were installed by the wealthy wool merchant, John Tame, when Fairford was a prosperous wool-producing centre. The set of 28 windows is believed to have been made by Henry VII's master glass painter, Barnard Flower, who is known for his work in Westminster Abbey. St Mary's also contains some fine oak carving, most notably the ceiling supports which are fashioned in the shape of angels. John Tame's memorial gravestone, along with those of his wife and son, are set into the floor of the church.

Church of St Mary the Blessed Virgin, Fairford

LECHLADE

Standing at the junction of the A417 and A361, Lechlade can be a busy place with wide streets and a bustling marketplace. It also stands at the point where the rivers Leach, from which the town gets its name, and Coln join the River Thames. **Halfpenny Bridge**, the highest navigable point on the river, is so-called because of the halfpenny toll which was once payable. At one time, river barges used to line the wharves around **St John's Bridge**, where they were loaded with building stone bound for Oxford, London and beyond. Today, the barges have been replaced by pleasure craft which provide an enjoyable change from the car, coach or cycle.

Lechlade contains some fine Georgian buildings, many of which were designed by an accomplished local architect called Pace. One of the most attractive and characteristic features of the town can be seen in the gardens of some of the older houses. Now much-prized, these unique gazebos were the highly fashionable garden accessories of their day. One such structure in the garden of **Church House** is said to be the place where Shelley wrote his *Stanzas in Lechlade Churchyard* in 1815. The

Church itself has a tall spire, which can be seen from miles away across the low surrounding water meadows, and an unusual carved roof boss depicting two wrestlers which can be seen inside above the nave.

SOUTHROP

The network of country lanes to the north of Lechlade connect a number of interesting little villages. Southrop is an attractive and beautifully kept community with a small green and a fine manor house. The manor is set behind a pair of impressive gateposts in grounds containing a restored riverside mill, ancient barns and a charming church with Norman features. John Keble lived in the Old Vicarage from 1823-25 during the period he was laying the foundations of the Oxford Movement with William Wilberforce and others. Southrop is also noted for the distinctive stone ball-finials which adorn many of the older buildings in the village.

EASTLEACH

A little further north, the hamlets of **Eastleach Martin** and **Eastleach Turville** face each other across the River Leach; together they form the village known simply as Eastleach. For many centuries, the two hamlets were owned by rival lords of the manor and so each has its own church. These date from Norman times and incorporate a number of fine architectural features. John Keble was appointed non-resident curate of both churches in 1815, and the ancient clapper footbridge across the River Leach which connects the two hamlets is still known as **Keble's Bridge**.

HATHEROP

Lying to the west of Eastleach, this is a pretty model village of solidly-built stone cottages which was constructed in the 1860s between the estates of Williamstrip Park and Hatherop Castle, the latter of which is now a girls' school. The Victorian village **Church** contains the chapel of Barbara, Lady de Maulay, which was designed by William Burges. He was also jointly responsible for remodelling the castle in the 1850s.

QUENINGTON

On the banks of the River Coln one mile to the southwest, the village of Quenington has a **Church** with two exceptional Norman tympana above the doors. Such is their importance that, in the 1880s, a pair of porches were added by the architect of Gloucester Cathedral, FS Waller, to protect them from the elements. In the 12th century, the Church became a preceptory of the Knights Hospitaller and the presence of the order is reflected in several local place names, including Knights' Mill and Knights' Gatehouse.

BIBURY

The picturesque village of Bibury lies three miles to the northwest of Quenington, at the point where the B4425 bridges the River Coln. In the 19th century, it was described by William Morris as 'the most beautiful village in England'. Thankfully, little has changed since then. The village square at its centre is overlooked by the ancient **Church of St Mary**, a much altered building which incorporates Saxon, Norman and medieval parts. Most of the lichen-speckled tombs and gravestones in the churchyard date from more recent times, their brilliant yellow mottle standing out in the clear Cotswold air.

The handsome stone-tiled buildings on either side of the slow-flowing River Coln are connected by Bibury's 18th century road bridge. The river and its water meadows attract a wide variety of wildfowl, and the nearby National Trust-owned **Rack Isle Water Meadow** has been designated a bird sanctuary. **Arlington Row**, a superb small terrace of medieval stone cottages, stands close by. Originally built in the 14th century to house sheep, the cottages were converted into cloth-weaving workshops in the 17th century and are now under the protection of the National trust.

Arlington Mill

Fabric from here was supplied to nearby **Arlington Mill**, a water-powered fulling mill which stands on the site of a corn-mill mentioned in the Domesday Book. (Fulling was the process of cleansing and thickening woollen material by immersing it in water and beating it with mechanically-operated hammers.) Today, Arlington Mill is a fascinating museum which houses a collection of industrial artefacts, crafts and furniture, including items made in the William Morris workshops. There are seventeen display rooms in all, including a blacksmith's forge, a wheelwright's workshop and a number of machine rooms containing working machinery. (Open daily, 10.30am to 7pm between mid-March and mid-November, and weekends only during winter months.)

The **Bibury Trout Farm** can be found adjacent to Arlington Mill. Originally established as a trout hatchery as long ago as 1906, it has grown into a flourishing working farm which welcomes visitors all year round. There is also a farm shop offering fresh and smoked fish, plants and gifts. (Open daily, 9am (11am Sundays) to 6pm, all year round.)

In the 17th century, Bibury was a famous horse racing centre. At one time it had a famous racing club which was the oldest of its kind in the country, having been founded during the reign of Charles II. Much of the racing activity centred around **Bibury Court**, a splendid country house which was built on the site of Roman, Saxon and Norman remains. Now a hotel, the building still provides a focus for horse-riding activities. It also once belonged to the influential Sackville family who were involved in a famous law suit involving a contested will. The case lasted several decades and is said to have provided the background for Charles Dickens' vicious indictment of the legal profession, *Bleak House*.

ABLINGTON

To the north of Bibury, a series of beautiful unspoilt villages lie along the course of the River Coln. The first of these is Ablington, a community which was immortalised by J Arthur Gibbs in his chronicle of Victorian rural life *A Cotswold Village*. A high stone wall surrounds Gibbs' former home, an Elizabethan manor house which is set within extensive landscaped grounds. On the main doorway of the manor there are five delicately carved heads, one of which is of Queen Elizabeth herself. Another interesting building is the 17th century gabled **Ablington House** which is partly concealed behind a high dry-stone wall. Its iron gateway is guarded by two stone lions rampant brought from the Palace of Westminster.

CHEDWORTH

The village gives its name to one of the most impressive archeological sites in the area, the National Trust-owned Chedworth Roman Villa.

Chedworth village is made up of a number of simple stone-built houses and farms which are huddled together in the shallow valley between Pancake Hill and Chedworth Beacon. As well as a handsome Norman church with a castellated tower, it possesses a number of fine gabled buildings, including the Old Farm and Cromwell House, and two rows of attractive 18th century cottages known as Church Row and Ballingers Row.

Chedworth Roman Villa

Chedworth Roman Villa is situated in the wooded valley of the River Coln one mile north of the village. (In fact, it is more easily approached from the northeast via Yanworth.) The villa is thought to have been built between the mid-2nd and early 4th centuries AD, and was accidentally rediscovered by a gamekeeper in 1864. This prompted the owner of the land, Lord Elton, to organise a series of excavations which eventually revealed a complex series of rooms and buildings, including a remarkably sophisticated bath house incorporating separate steam and dry heat 'saunas', a pool for taking a cold plunge, and a system for circulating warm air underfloor.

A number of beautiful and richly-patterned mosaics were also uncovered, including one on the floor of the dining room which consists of eight panels decorated with nymphs and satyrs set around a central octagon; another superb mosaic depicts the four seasons. Another interesting feature is the shrine adorned with water nymphs which was built above the villa's fresh water spring.

The site was acquired by the National Trust in 1924 who have recently erected an impressive visitors' centre. A ten-minute video giving further background information on Chedworth Roman Villa can be viewed here. An earlier museum building dating from the 1860s houses a display of some of the smaller artefacts unearthed on the site. (Open daily 10am to 5.30pm, between March and end-October (closed Mondays except Bank Holidays), plus restricted winter opening hours.)

NORTHLEACH

This is an attractive former market town which is situated near the junction of the A40 and the A429 Fosse Way, four miles northeast of the Roman villa. In common with many other Gloucestershire communities, this was once a major wool-trading centre which at one time rivalled Cirencester in importance.

St Peter and St Paul, Northleach

As a consequence, it possesses a disproportionately large church, the

15th century **Church of St Peter and St Paul**, which is only outshone by those in Cirencester and Chipping Campden. Constructed in light Perpendicular style with pinnacled buttresses, high windows and a massive square castellated tower, the interior is noted for its ornately carved font and rare monumental brasses, some of the finest of their kind in the country. (Brass rubbing permits can be obtained from the Cotswold Pharmacy and the necessary materials from the post office.)

After a long period of decline caused the late-medieval downturn in the local wool industry, Northleach rose to become an important stopping point on the Gloucester to Oxford coaching route in the mid-18th century. In the 1780s, a house of correction was built near the old main crossroads which dealt out an early form of short sharp shock to offenders found guilty of minor crimes. The 37 inmates were kept in relatively good conditions - for example, they were allowed washing facilities - but were subjected to hard labour, including work on a treadmill.

The building has since been converted into a fascinating museum of rural life, the **Cotswold Countryside Collection**, whose exhibits include a courtroom and cell block restored to their original condition. The museum also houses the renowned collection of historic agricultural implements gathered by Olive Lloyd-Baker, a local woman with a special interest in the evolution of modern agriculture. Exhibits include a steam tractor, an early laundry and an interesting collection of below-the-stairs domestic items. (Open daily 10am (2pm Sundays) to 5pm between 1 April and 31 October.)

Another highly-entertaining museum, **Harding's World Of Mechanical Music**, is situated in a 17th century merchant's house in Northleach High Street. This unique attraction features a collection of antique music boxes, chiming clocks and mechanically-driven musical instruments which are played to visitors during guided tours and demonstrations. Proprietor Keith Harding also restores clocks and music boxes, and selects the items offered in the delightful on-site gift shop. (Open daily, 10am to 6pm, all year round.) Those interested in original works of art should make a point of finding Fothergill's Gallery in the High Street.

SHERBORNE

Lying in the lanes four miles to the east of Northleach, Sherborne is a delightful village of Cotswold stone houses which are strung out in twos and threes along the course of Sherborne Brook. In the centre of the village, a number of grander buildings surround **Sherborne House**, a classical country mansion rebuilt in 1830 which has now been turned into private flats. The nearby **Church of St Mary Magdalene** contains several impressive monuments to the local land-owning family, the Duttons. Sherborne is surrounded by picturesque National Trust-owned woodland which contains some lovely waymarked walks and scenic viewpoints.

LITTLE BARRINGTON

Situated in the shallow valley of the River Windrush, three miles further east, the idyllic sister villages of Great and Little Barrington were once an internationally renowned source of Cotswold limestone. Several of the Oxford colleges and the interior of St Paul's Cathedral in London were constructed of stone quarried here. Indeed, Wren considered Thomas Strong, the owner of the quarries at Little Barrington, to be the leading mason of his generation. For many years, river barges were loaded with stone at a wharf near the Fox Inn which were then floated down the Windrush and the Thames to London. Thomas Strong left money in his will to build the stone causeway across the river which can still be seen nearby. Today, the Barringtons are peaceful villages built of indigenous Cotswold stone which create an idyllic, if somewhat feudal, picture of English rural life.

BOURTON-ON-THE-WATER

From Great Barrington, a minor country road follows the course of the River Windrush upstream through Great Rissington to Bourton-on-the-Water, one of the most popular attractions in the Cotswolds. Despite its regular influx of visitors, this sizable village still manages to retain a magical feel. The shallow Windrush flows through heart of the village under a series of charming low-arched pedestrian bridges, two of which date from the late 18th century. The riverside is lined with willowed greens from which narrow lanes run back between golden Cotswold stone cottages. In Sherborne Street, look out for the unusual dovecotes built into the walls. There are also some fine larger buildings, including **St Lawrence's Church** with its 14th century chancel and Georgian tower, and the Old Manse dating from 1784 which has since been converted into a hotel.

Bourton-on-the-Water

Bourton-on-the-Water also contains some interesting attractions which are worth a visit, particularly if the weather is unreliable. **Birdland** is a remarkable three-and-a-half acre private zoological garden which is situated within the grounds of a Tudor manor house. It was founded in 1956 by local builder, Leonard Hill, to realise his dream of creating a living sanctuary for exotic birds of all descriptions. Today, the gardens are filled with aviaries, ponds and densely-treed groves which are home to over a thousand brightly plumaged birds. Macaws and parrots fly freely in the open, sunbirds and hummingbirds flit about the tropical houses, toucans and flamingos inhabit the aviaries, and penguins swim in a glass-sided pool. (Open daily all year round.)

The gardens behind the enigmatically named Old New Inn in the High Street are the location of another of Bourton-on-the-Water's attractions, its famous **Model Village**. During the 1930s, the present landlord's father, helped by a team of skilled craftspeople, built a one-ninth scale replica of the village complete with inn, church, shops, flowing River Windrush and working water wheel. All the buildings are made of Cotswold stone, and there is even a miniature version of the Model Village itself. (Open daily all year round.)

The **Cotswold Motor Museum and Toy Collection** occupies an 18th century water-mill in Sherborne Street. In addition to the 30 or so cars and motorcycles on show, the museum contains a fascinating range of memorabilia, including a collection of antique children's toys and the largest display of historic advertising signs in the country. (Open daily 10am to 6pm between February and November.) Those interested in model railways should also make a point of finding the **Bourton Model Railway** in the High Street, where over 40 British and overseas trains run on over 400 feet of track in three different gauges. (Open daily between April and September, and weekends only in winter.) Bourton-on-the-Water also contains Europe's only **Perfumery Exhibition**, a permanent attraction which includes an explanation of the extraction process, an audio visual show in a specially constructed 'smelly vision' theatre, and an attractive perfume garden filled with fragrant plants. (Open daily, all year round.)

The renowned **Folly Farm** waterfowl and garden centre can be found three miles outside Bourton-on-the-Water off the A436 Cheltenham road. This interesting conservation farm contains one of the largest private collections of rare domestic waterfowl in Europe. It was started before World War II by Tom Bartlett, a recognised expert in his field who has written and broadcast on the subject throughout his life. The visitor area now covers over 50 acres and is home to over 160 breeds of birds and small animals, many of them novel and exotic. (Open daily 10am to 6pm (4pm in winter), all year round.)

UPPER AND LOWER SLAUGHTER

Situated only a couple of miles north of Bourton-on-the-Water yet entirely different in character are the twin villages known collectively as the Slaughters. Despite their gruesome connotations, the settlements actually take their name from the innocuous Anglo-Saxon word, *slohtre*, meaning 'muddy place'. Set a mile apart and joined by the River Eye, Upper and Lower Slaughter are archetypal Cotswold villages. Each consists of a cluster of honey-coloured limestone buildings set around a church and manor. Apart from some renovation to cottages in Baghot's Square by Sir Edwin Lutyens in 1906, no new buildings have been constructed in Upper Slaughter since 1904. Francis Edward Witts, whose *Diary Of A Cotswold Parson* was published in 1978, was the rector here from 1808 to 1854. Both villages are very photogenic and best explored on foot.

The **Old Mill** at Lower Slaughter is a restored 19th century flour mill with a giant water wheel which stands on the banks of the River Eye. This fascinating building provides an interesting insight into the operation of a Victorian flour mill, and also incorporates a popular tearoom and ice cream parlour. (Open daily, 10am to 6pm, all year round.)

The Old Mill, Lower Slaughter

NAUNTON

Its worth making a detour off the B4068 Cheltenham to Stow-on-the-Wold road to visit Naunton, an exceptional community which looks like a village in miniature from the road running along the top of the ridge. It was founded in Saxon times and features a 14th century church and a string of characteristic stone cottages which are congregated on either side of the upper River Windrush. According to local legend, Naunton's first inhabitant was an imp who fell to earth and broke a wing when flying over the Cotswolds with his satanic master. Finding himself unable to fly, he decided to build himself a cottage of local stone and took up residence.

STOW-ON-THE-WOLD

At 800 feet above sea level, Stow-on-the-Wold is the highest town in the Cotswolds. Eight roads converge near the town, although fortunately only one actually passes through its centre. Instead, Stow survives as an exceptional collection of 17th and 18th century stone houses clustered around a market cross. Two of its main thoroughfares are called Sheep Street and Shepherds Way, reminders of the days when the town's main economic activity was wool trading.

At one time, large twice-yearly sheep fairs were held on Stow's open Market Square, and an absorbing first-hand account of one such event was written by Daniel Defoe. The square is also the site of the town stocks which once were used for punishing minor offenders. Narrow alleys, or *tures*, radiate from here which were used on market days for counting sheep in single file. Eventually, the sheep fairs were replaced by an annual horse fair which continued until 1985.

Stow's **Church of St Edward** was named after the unfortunate King Edward the Martyr who was murdered at Corfe Castle by his wicked stepmother, Elfrida. It has been restored on a number of occasions over the centuries and is now considered one of the outstanding Cotswold churches. It also contains a famous 17th century painting of the Crucifixion by Gaspard de Craeyer of Antwerp. Other noteworthy buildings in the town include the 15th century **Crooked House**, now an antique shop, the 16th century **Masonic Hall**, and the 18th century **Talbot** which was once the local corn exchange.

Stow-on-the-Wold

During the English Civil War, Stow-on-the-Wold was considered to be of great strategic importance and forces from both sides regularly passed through. On 21st March 1646, a hilltop to the northwest of the town was the site of the last open battle of the first Civil War. Afterwards, the defeated Royalist forces withdrew into the streets of the town and some were fortunate enough to reach the relative safety of St Edward's Church. Others, however, were cut down in the Market Square and according to local reports, ducks were seen bathing in the blood which flowed through the streets. One Royalist officer, Captain Keyte, is buried beneath a slate slab in the chancel of the church.

CONDICOTE

The area further to the northwest around Condicote contains some interesting archeological remains, including those of the Roman **Ryknild Street**, the imposing Iron Age fortification known as **Eubury Camp**, and the site of a prehistoric henge dating from around 2500 BC.

ADLESTROP

The delightful village of Adlestrop lies to the north of the A436 Chipping Norton road, three miles east of Stow-on-the-Wold. Another Cotswold gem, it is filled with honey-coloured cottages and boasts a Georgian mansion, a 13th century church and a 17th century rectory. The mansion, **Adlestrop Park**, was built in Gothic style with grounds laid out by Humphry Repton; sadly, neither are open to the public. The **Church of St Mary Magdalene** contains several memorials to the Leigh family, owners of Adlestrop Park since 1553. Jane Austen's grandfather, Thomas Leigh, was incumbent here for many years and the author was a regular visitor to the rectory, which stands surrounded by mature cedar trees near a 19th century school house and cottage.

Adlestrop is perhaps best-known, however, for being the title of a poem by Edward Thomas, a great admirer of the English countryside who was killed in action during the First World War. The work was written on a train following a brief halt at the now-demolished Adlestrop station (which incidentally was situated some distance away from the village). The station nameplate which fired Thomas' imagination can now been seen in the village bus shelter along with a plaque inscribed with his famous poem.

EVENLODE

To the north of Adlestrop, a minor country road leads through the quiet Cotswold village of Evenlode. A two-mile walk to the east of here leads to **Chastleton House**, a magnificent country mansion which has remained virtually unchanged since it was constructed in 1603. The interior contains some elegant period furniture and a secret room where a

Royalist family is said to have been concealed during the English Civil War. The nearby garden contains some amusing examples of box topiary.

MORETON-IN-MARSH

Continuing northwards, Moreton-in-Marsh is a bustling market town which stands at the busy junction of the A44 and the A429 Fosse Way. Unlike many similar communities in the Cotswolds which were dependent on the wool trade, Moreton managed to flourish in the late-medieval period by becoming a leading linen-weaving centre. Later, it became an important stopping place for stagecoaches travelling between London and the West Midlands.

The centre of present day Moreton-in-Marsh is full of handsome 18th and 19th century buildings which create a pleasant period atmosphere. A small number of structures date from an earlier era; these include the old town gaol and the unusual **Curfew Tower** with its bell dated 1633 which in its time has been used to summon the local fire brigade. Like Stow-on-the-Wold, Moreton-in-Marsh was strategically important during the English Civil War and King Charles I himself is reported to have stayed at the White Hart Inn during one fleeting visit.

Moreton-in-Marsh contains two interesting specialist museums. The **Bygones Museum** at Aston Magna contains an unusual display of historic farm implements and folk memorabilia. (Open Wednesdays and Sundays between Easter and end-October.) The **Wellington Aviation Art Museum** in Broadway Road contains a unique collection of World War II aircraft paintings, prints and models, together with details of the aircraft's historical background. (Open Tuesdays to Sundays, 10am to 12.30pm and 2.30pm to 5.30pm.)

BATSFORD

Situated in the lanes to the northwest of Moreton-in-Marsh, the **Cotswold Falconry Centre** at Batsford provides a rare opportunity to observe falcons, eagles, hawks and owls in flight. Birds are flown throughout the day, providing visitors with a chance to appreciate their speed, agility and grace. There are also several pairs of breeding birds, including the owls in 'Owl Wood'. (Open daily between 1 March and 31 October, plus weekend until Christmas.)

Almshouses, Chipping Campden

The Market Hall, Chipping Campden

BOURTON-ON-THE-HILL

The aptly-named Bourton-on-the-Hill stands at the top of a steep rise, two miles along the A44 to the west of Moreton-in-Marsh. This pleasant village has a fine part-Norman church and a mansion, **Bourton House**, which is surrounded by beautiful landscaped grounds containing a 16th century tithe barn.

Another impressive country house and garden can be found a mile to the south of here, the highly eccentric **Sezincote**. In 1805, this unusual house was rebuilt for a director of the East India Company, Sir Charles Cockerell, by his architect brother. He was assisted in his task by the noted Indian artist Thomas Daniell whose influence led to such distinctive features as its copper-covered onion-shaped dome. This was once brightly burnished, but is now coated in thick blue-green verdigris. Sezincote was visited in 1807 by the future Prince Regent and its design is said to have provided the inspiration for Brighton Pavilion. The grounds contain a number of features similarly inspired by the Indian subcontinent, including a wonderful water-garden laid out by Repton and Daniell. (House open 2.30pm to 5.30pm on Thursdays and Fridays during May, June, July and September; gardens open 2pm to 6pm on Thursdays and Fridays all year round except December, plus Bank Holidays and selected Sundays.)

BLOCKLEY

The village lies on the B4479, a mile-and-a-half to the north of Bourton-on-the-Hill. Despite its present unspoilt appearance, this attractive settlement has had an unexpectedly diverse industrial past. The fast-flowing Blockley Brook is fed by an unusual number of local springs and as a consequence, the village became a popular site for water-powered mills. Indeed, as many as a dozen were recorded here in the Domesday Book at the end of the 11th century. In medieval times, Blockley's main industrial activity was silk spinning, the output from which mostly went to the ribbon weavers of Coventry, though at one time, the village also boasted an iron foundry and factories making soap, collars and even pianos. Today, the silk mills have been converted into desirable private homes and the village has an air of secluded wellbeing.

Blockley experienced a brief period of notoriety in the early 19th century as the home of Joanna Southcott, a religious fanatic who claimed she would give birth to the second Messiah. Following a series of disturbances in the village, her house was burnt to the ground. Southcott eventually died of a brain disease, although her following lasted into the 20th century. Today, the rebuilt **Rock Cottage** is marked with a commemorative plaque attached to two sturdy gateposts. Blockley is also the location of **Sleepy Hollow Farm Park**, an open farm with an interesting collection of rare and unusual farm animals, including Shire horses and otters. (Open daily, late March to late October.)

CHIPPING CAMPDEN

Three miles further north, Chipping Campden is a picturesque community of early gabled buildings which has remained largely unaltered for centuries. More a large village than a town, it was a regional capital of the wool-trade between the 13th and 16th centuries, and many of the fine buildings which can be seen here today date from this era of prosperity. (Chipping, a name occurring several times in the Cotswolds, is derived from the Old English word meaning 'market' or 'trading centre'.) The Perpendicular 15th century **Church of St James**, with its magnificent 120 foot pinnacled tower, is considered the finest wool church in the Cotswolds after Cirencester. The interior contains a number of impressive monumental brasses, including one of William Grevel which at 8 feet by 4 feet is thought to be the largest in the country. Its Latin inscription reads, 'the flower of the wool merchants of all England'. Also on view is a glass display case containing a rare collection of embroidery, including an example dating back to the time of Richard II.

The noted 17th century wool merchant and financier, Sir Baptist Hicks, was responsible for many of the finer Cotswold-stone buildings in the village, including the Jacobean **Market Hall**. Completed around 1627, this unique structure can be recognised by its steeply-pitched gable ends and open arcade. Fifteen years before, he endowed a group of charming almshouses which were laid out in the shape of the letter 'I' in honour of King James I, or 'Iacobus' in the Latin of the time. Hicks was also responsible for building what was the largest residence in the village of its day. During the English Civil War, however, Old Campden House was burned to the ground by Royalists to prevent it falling into the hands of the enemy. The only surviving remains are two unusual gatehouses near the Church, and the old stable block which was subsequently converted to a dower house. Towards the end of his career, Hicks is said to have been so rich that even the King asked to borrow money from him.

Another interesting character from Chipping Campden's past is William Harrison, an elderly rent collector who vanished in 1660. A woman and two of her sons were accused of his murder and hanged. Two years later, however, Harrison, the 'Campden Wonder', turned up in the village proclaiming a story of kidnapping, robbery and Turkish pirates.

Woolstaplers' Hall, Chipping Campden

Chipping Campden's many attractions include the town hall, Grevel House, and the Ernest Wilson memorial garden with its collection of Chinese and Japanese botanical specimens. Also in the High Street is the **Woolstaplers' Hall**, a 14th century merchant's house which is now an interesting museum. Its eleven rooms contain a diverse collection of historic memorabilia, including domestic items, cameras, office equipment, clothing and an apothecary's shop. (Open daily, 11am to 6pm between 1 April to 31 October.)

Between 1612 and the mid-19th century, the natural amphitheatre above Chipping Campden known as **Dover's Hill** hosted an annual series of organised games. In part, these so-called 'Olimpick Games' followed the traditions of Ancient Greece; however, they also involved more colloquial activities such as shin-kicking and bare-knuckle fighting. After having survived for almost 250 years, the increasing lawlessness and hooliganism surrounding the games led magistrates to close them down in 1852.

However in 1951, they were revived in a modern form and each year on the Friday following the spring Bank Holiday, a series of competitions takes place which ends with a spectacular torchlight procession.

EBRINGTON

Lying to the north of the B4035 Banbury road, two miles east of Chipping Campden, the village of Ebrington is a quintessential Cotswold community of honey-coloured buildings with neat thatched roofs. On one side, the village falls away in irregular steps into a valley filled with apple and cherry orchards. There was a manor here as early as the 13th century, although the present manor house dates from around 400 years later. The village **Church of St Eadburgha** contains a number of early features, including a Saxon stone coffin, a Norman nave and a medieval tower. It also has an unusual 17th century pulpit and a statue of Sir John Fortescue wearing the full regalia of a mid-15th century Lord Chief Justice.

HIDCOTE BARTRIM

The network of country lanes to the north of Ebrington leads to Motor Museum, Bourton-on-the-Waterand Birdland, Bourton-on-the-Water, home of the beautiful National Trust-owned **Hidcote Manor Garden**. One of the most acclaimed 20th century gardens in the UK, it was begun in 1907 by an American army officer, Major Lawrence Johnston, who set out to transform the exposed Cotswold escarpment into a series of delightful enclosed gardens. The only original features were a copse of mature beech trees, a lone cedar of Lebanon, and a stream which flowed through a small valley. After creating a number of wide terraces, Johnston planted a succession of protective hedges composed of contrasting plant types, for example, yellow-leaved yew was interspersed with dark-leaved yew, and copper beech with standard beech.

This created a series of sheltered compartments which he then filled with plants and shrubs, usually according to a recognisable theme, for example, some compartments have flowers or foliage of the same colour, others a common plant type. The water garden is less formal and consists of a rambling path overhung with trees which winds along the course of the stream between species shrubs and moisture-loving plants. There is also a large kitchen garden near the house whose walls are covered in clematis and old-fashioned climbing roses. (Open daily, except Tuesdays and Fridays, 11am to 7pm between April and end-October.) In summer,

Hidecote Manor Garden provides a beautiful setting for outdoor performances of Shakespeare's plays.

Another attractive garden, **Kiftsgate Court**, can be found nearby which features a wide range of less well-known flora, including tree peonies and oldfashioned roses. (Open Sundays, Wednesdays and Thursdays between 1 April and 30 September.)

CHAPTER SIX
Oxford Cotswolds

Cotswold Wildlife Park, Nr Burford

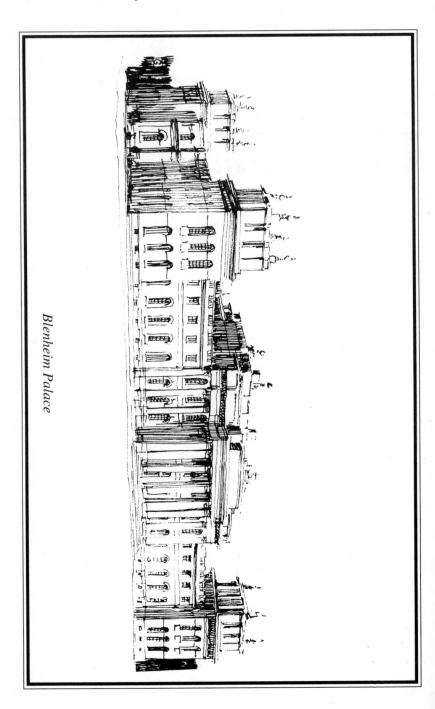

Blenheim Palace

6
Oxford Cotswolds

WOODSTOCK

John Churchill (1650-1722), 1st Duke of Marlborough, was a brave soldier, skilful general and had, as we say nowadays, an eye on the main chance. And if he had lacked anything in this faculty it would have been more than made up for by his wife, Sarah. He was also, we are told, an even-tempered man and a loving husband and father, who was always concerned about the welfare of his troops. At the height of his power after the victory at Blenheim during the War of the Spanish Succession, he was received in London as a hero and Queen Anne proposed that he should be rewarded with a Palace. She gave him her manor at Woodstock as the site, but there the national gratitude seems to have run out of steam, for he paid for most of it himself in the end.

As his architect, Marlborough chose Sir John Vanbrugh whose life was even more colourful than that of his patron. He was at the same time both an architect (although at the time he was relatively unknown as such) and a playwright, and had the distinction of having been imprisoned in the Bastille. The result of his work was the Continental-looking baroque **Blenheim Palace**, which we now see set in a very English park laid out later by Capability Brown. The new house did not meet with universal approval. It was ridiculed by Jonathan Swift and Alexander Pope; Duchess Sarah, who seems to have held the family purse strings, delayed paying Vanbrugh as long as possible. But recently its international importance has been recognised by inclusion in the UNESCO World Heritage List.

It is a magnificent Palace, both inside and out, and, after marvelling at the treasures and the more intimate souvenirs of Marlborough's descendant, Sir Winston Churchill, visitors can enjoy a refreshing walk through the formal gardens and park. The Blenheim Orange apple got its name from here. It was first grown by George Kempster, a tailor from Old Woodstock. The exact date of the first apple is unknown. Kempster himself died in 1773 and the original tree blew down in 1853. A plaque in Old Woodstock marks its site. So famous did the spot become that it is said London-bound coaches and horses used to slow down so that passengers might gaze upon it.

Woodstock itself is a relaxed, unpretentious place giving no hint of the grandeur of its most famous building, which is approached through the main street. It has a much longer history than does Blenheim, however. It was formerly the centre of the glove making industry and was the site of one of the most splendid of the medieval royal Palaces, the scene of Henry II's courtship of 'the Fair Rosamond', and birthplace of the Black Prince. Elizabeth I was imprisoned there in 1554 by her sister, Mary Tudor. The old Palace was damaged during the Civil War, when it served as a Royalist garrison and the last remains were demolished in 1710.

The Church is interesting. The original medieval building was practically rebuilt in Victorian times, but the tower is classical, built in 1785.

Vanbrughs Coffee House, 16 Oxford Street, Woodstock
Tel: 01933 811253

John Vanbrugh was born in London in 1664 and is now most famous for his great contribution to British architecture giving us Castle Howard near York as well as Blenheim Palace. It is from this famous location and its connections that **Vanbrughs Coffee House** takes its name. Indeed it is believed that Vanbrugh stayed in this house whilst the Palace was being built.

Setting their own standards in healthy eating by participating in West Oxfordshire Environmental Health Department's Heartbeat Award, Vanbrughs Coffee House offers a Healthy Options Menu. Throughout the day a selection of imaginatively-prepared interesting dishes are served, anything from breakfast, coffee and pastries and light snacks to 'Woodstock Platters' with selections from the Deli counter, accompanied perhaps by a glass of wine. Lean ground Beef Burgers, sandwiches and cream teas are also on the menu. A tempting selection of concoctions from the ice cream parlour may prove to be too much, so be prepared to spoil yourself!

BLADON

Heading south from Woodstock along the A34 south and turning off onto the A4095 brings us to Bladon and the Churchyard where Sir Winston Churchill lies, together with other members of his family. The Churchyard, on the edge of the park, has become a place of modern pilgrimage.

The village is on what must be one of the most evocatively-named of all English rivers, the Evenlode. We are now, of course, in the Cotswolds, that much loved part of England for which the phrase 'green and pleasant land' might have been coined.

NORTH LEIGH

Continue along the A4095, turning northwestwards up the delightful valley of the Evenlode in search of the **Roman Villa** at North Leigh. We last met the Romans around Bicester, and here they are again as we loop up to cross, once more, the line of Akeman Street as it runs southwest to meet the Fosse Way coming up from Bath towards the north.

The villa, one of several known to have existed in the vicinity, is at **East End** just outside the village of North Leigh itself. It was large, with over 60 rooms, two sets of baths, an under-floor heating system and mosaic pavements including one with attractive interlaced patterns. The site is known to have been occupied by Romans from the 1st century AD, but the house, which is built around a courtyard, reached its present form in the 4th century, when it was clearly the home of a prosperous farming family and their servants, able to 'export' their produce using the transport opportunities offered by Akeman Street.

Before leaving North Leigh, the Church is well worth a visit; it has a Saxon tower, and there is the small 15th century Wilcote Chapel, built by Elizabeth Wilcote in memory of her two husbands and two sons, with intricate fan vaulting.

STONESFIELD

Having travelled through time from the Romans to a great leader of our own century, evidence of even older inhabitants has been found at Stonesfield. At a nearby quarry a geology student discovered the fossilised remains of the earliest known stegosaurus. These were fearsome looking dinosaurs, with lashing tails armed with spikes, who lived in the area some 160 million years ago. It seems hard to imagine them roaming through the peaceful landscape we see today.

The name of the village, incidentally, has nothing to do with quarries or the local stone, but is derived from Stunt's or Stunta's field - Stunt being a nickname from the Old English word for foolish!

FINSTOCK

The Plough Inn at The Bottom can truly be described as a family-run inn for the family. Margaret, Sue, Keith and Nigel all pull together to make it happen at the Plough. Here you will find log fires ablaze and many stuffed animals and birds keeping a watchful eye from their assigned positions. Built around 1772, The Plough Inn was first a farmer's cottage which later became a private dwelling and subsequently a pub called The Churchill in 1804; it was the first country inn to be owned by Halls Brewery. Copies of the original documents of the signing of the freehold are displayed on the walls of this lovely atmospheric pub.

There's a great welcome for everyone at this pub, babies, prams, pushchairs, dogs - all are welcome. The owners are great dog lovers and two champion canines are resident on the premises; many winning rosettes are displayed on the low beams. The inn is close to Wychwood Forest popular with walkers and cyclists; five walks have their starting point at the Plough. Many claims of ghost sightings are made by the villagers including Urchins, believed to be from Roman times, throwing stones in the village. A great place to make for with the reward of great hospitality, traditional home cooked food and some great ales.

The Plough Inn, The Bottom, Finstock Tel: 01933 868333

ENSTONE

Next we take the B4437 into **Charlbury**, a pleasant stone-built town, then the B4022 towards Enstone to visit **Ditchley Park**. The building of the house was begun about 1720 and was designed by James Gibbs in a restrained classical style. The interiors are splendid, having been designed by William Kent and Henry Flitcroft. Italian craftsmen worked on the stucco decorations of the great hall and the saloon, the first treated to give an impression of rich solemnity, the second with a rather more exuberant effect.

The house has associations with Sir Winston Churchill, who used it as a weekend headquarters during the 1939-45 War. Appropriately enough, given that Sir Winston had an American mother, Ditchley Park is now used as an Anglo-American conference centre.

CHIPPING NORTON

Chipping Norton is a lovely town, at the centre of the Evenlode valley's prosperous wool trade in medieval times, based on sheep which grazed the Cotswolds.

This wealth is reflected in the fine Church, where the Nave, built about 1485, is flooded with light from the clerestory and east window. The latter originally came from the Abbey of Bruern, a few miles to the south west, which was demolished in 1535 during the dissolution of the monasteries under Henry VIII.

The 'Chipping' part of the town's name comes from the Old English word for 'market' (the same word, incidentally, is the origin of the 'cheap' in Cheapside in London) and fittingly it has a fine market place. The surrounding streets more than repay a little wander, as there are many intriguing houses, including some attractive 17th century almshouses.

CHURCHILL

Next we take the B4450 towards the village of Churchill. The 'father of British geology', William Smith (1769-1839) was born in this village. He began his professional life as a canal engineer, and went on to work out the method of telling the age of geological strata by the fossils found in them. In 1815 he published a geological map of England, the first of its kind. There is a memorial to him, an impressive monolith of local stone.

Less well served as far as memorials are concerned is James Langton, whose daughter erected a fountain in his memory here in 1870. This is, as the Buildings of England volume on Oxfordshire put it, 'memorably ugly'. However, the villagers may well have been grateful for it in the days before mains water and taps in every home.

Warren Hastings, who administered India on behalf of the East India Company from 1773 until 1784 was also born in this village. His is a vivid story, as colourful as India itself, full of intrigue, wars, corruption and allegations of corruption. In Hastings' own case such charges led to him being impeached before the House of Lords, and a trial which dragged on for seven years.

Eventually he was personally vindicated and retired to be a country gentleman in Daylesford, not far from his birthplace. His house there had been his family home; buying it and living in it was for him the fulfilment of an ambition he had had since childhood.

BLEDINGTON

At Bledington the village green is complete with brook and ducks - all

The Sundial Signpost, near Chipping Norton

known locally by name.

LONG COMPTON

Next we turn towards Long Compton in order to find, a little to the south, reminders of rather less urbane times, the prehistoric stone circle known as the **Rollright Stones**. These great knarled fists of stone stand on a ridge giving fine views of the surrounding countryside. They all have nicknames - the King's Men form a circle, the King Stone is to the north of the circle and a quarter of a mile to the west stand the Whispering Knights, which are in fact the remnants of a megalithic tomb which has lost its original covering mound of earth. Visitors soaking in the sense of the mysterious which these ancient stones seem to possess can only guess at their original purpose.

MILTON-UNDER-WYCHWOOD

Our next stop is to be Milton-under-Wychwood, which sits right in the middle of the square formed by Moreton-in-Marsh, Chipping Norton, Burford and Stow-in-the-Wold, but the easiest way to reach it is to take the A361 from Burford towards Chipping Norton. About a third of the way along the road you will come to Shipton-under-Wychwood where a signposted left turn will take you to Milton.

There are architectural styles of many different periods throughout Oxfordshire and Milton is no exception, having a school, teacher's house and Church designed by the prominent Victorian architect GE Street in 1853-4. The Church is a good example of Street's early Gothic style and has a lychgate. Together the buildings make an attractive group.

What better way to spend a summer afternoon than watching a game of cricket on the village green. The Wychwoods nestle deeply into the beautiful Evenlode Valley where you can walk in the most glorious scenery.

SHIPTON-UNDER-WYCHWOOD

Next we explore Milton's neighbour, Shipton-under-Wychwood, which has a number of interesting buildings. The Church, which was begun about 1200, has a 14th century porch with a relief of the Annunciation over the entrance showing the Virgin in elegant drapery.

Shipton Court was built about 1603. The front is elegant and well proportioned with five narrow gables but the overall lack of symmetry in the plan suggests that the house was based on an earlier one. The house was completely remodelled internally in a restoration carried out in the early years of this century. Among other buildings well worth a look is the **Shaven Crown Inn**, which dates from the 15th century.

The suffix 'under-Wychwood' derives from the Wychwood, which was an ancient royal hunting forest, much larger than the remnant of woodland near Charlbury. The name has nothing to do with witches - 'wych' refers to the Hwicce, a Celtic tribe of whose territory the forest originally formed a part.

The forest was one of the alleged haunts of Matthew Arnold's 'scholar gypsy'. In the poem, published in 1853, Arnold tells the legend of the brilliant but poor Oxford scholar who, despairing of ever making his way in the world, went to live with the gypsies to learn from their way of life, and for long after could sometimes be seen *'leaning backward in a pensive dream, And fostering in thy lap a heap of flowers Pluck'd in shy fields and distant Wychwood bowers, And thine eyes resting on the moonlit stream ...'.*

The distant Wychwood bowers are much less accessible now. The wood was for a long time completely closed to the public, but protracted negotiations have resulted in the opening of one footpath, leading into the forest just north of the village of **Leafield**, south east of Shipton-under-Wychwood.

TAYNTON

We resume our journey by way of minor roads towards Burford, passing through the village where the great Victorian polymath, William Morris spent his summers, Taynton. The stone for Blenheim Palace, most of the Oxford Colleges, Windsor Castle and St Paul's Cathedral was taken from nearby quarries. The village itself is a charming huddle of stone-built thatched cottages grouped around an interesting Church which has a Perpendicular tower.

BURFORD

The honey-coloured Cotswold stone of Burford and its setting on the river Windrush (the name derived, apparently, from the prosaic 'white marsh') make it an unforgettable composition. When William Morris, revolted by the dirt and stench of Victorian London, wrote *'and dream of*

London, small and white and clean, the clear Thames bordered by its gardens green' it is quite easy to imagine Burford, or somewhere very similar, hovering at the back of his mind.

The wool of the Cotswolds, once again, brought Burford its medieval prosperity and today we can see the result in the houses of the wool merchants which still remain. By the beginning of the 15th century it was already one of the leading wool markets, its wealthy heyday lasting until the early 16th. After that it declined, though it remained an important coaching centre with several large inns throughout the 18th century.

After the main road to London and then the railway bypassed the town, it became a backwater until the tourist trade of this century revived its fortunes. What we enjoy so much rests on the fact of it having remained impervious to the progressive modernisation suffered by other towns.

Compton Mackenzie, who lived for a time in Burford before the 1914-1918 War, wrote about the town as 'Wychford' in his novel *Guy and Pauline*, which was published in 1915.

The Church is one of its great glories, the original Norman building having been added to over the centuries so that it gives the impression of having 'just growed'.

In 1649 it was the scene of the last act of a tragic aftermath of the Civil War. Troops from Cromwell's army who were representatives of the most democratic strand of thought in the Parliamentary army, known as Levellers, mutinied against what they saw as the drift towards the authoritarian rule they had been fighting to root out. While they were encamped in Burford, they were taken by surprise by Cromwell's forces. After a brief fight 340 prisoners were taken and placed under guard in the Church. The next day there was a court martial and three of the rebels were shot as an example to the rest, who were made to watch the execution.

Robert and Jayne Lewin invite you to explore the natural beauty of solid wood in their showroom at **Burford Woodcraft** in the High Street. Items are carefully chosen from the best the craftsmen create to offer a wide range, where the emphasis is on good design and quality of finish. Robert is one of the 50 talented British craftsmen whose work is displayed in the attractive showroom. By using a variety of techniques and finishes they hand-craft high quality furniture and products which complement the natural vitality of wood. If you are looking for original gift ideas, however modest or grand, there is much to delight and intrigue, not only the practical - furniture, lamps, clocks and bowls - but the creative - wonderful boxes to keep treasures safe. There are also carved birds, jewellery and one-off original pieces plus much much more including toys, mirrors and photoframes. Burford Woodcraft will welcome you with a friendly personal service.

Burford Woodcraft, 144 High Street, Burford Tel: 01993 823479

Burford House is not difficult to find, being on the main street right in the heart of this picturesque place. The frontage of the hotel, whilst being quite beautiful itself, hides many delightful secrets. The oldest part of the hotel dates back to the 15th century and there are many outstanding features, from original mullioned windows to stone fireplaces and low beamed ceilings. The house invites you to retire from the hustle and bustle to the peace and tranquillity to be found inside, in the cosy sitting rooms where a log fire burns in autumn and winter, and in the delightful flower-filled courtyard in the spring and summer. During the day, morning coffee and crumpets, light lunches and cream teas are served as well as aperitifs or something stronger should you desire.

Burford House Hotel, 99 High Street, Burford Tel: 01993 823151

Owned and run by Jane and Simon Henty who previously managed a Country House Hotel for the owners of the world famous Reids Hotel in Madeira, Burford House justifiably earns its AA 5Q Premier Select Award, the top rating for small hotels and inns. Furnished to the highest degree of tradition and comfort, the hotel offers seven individually styled bedrooms all en-suite and some with beautiful four poster beds and grand Victorian bathtubs. In each room will be found a traditional English Teddy Bear. The rooms are named after the local villages and hamlets.

One should appreciate that Burford House is also the home of the owners, reflected in the many personal touches to be seen around the hotel. Should you wish to move beyond the lovely town, which itself has a wealth of restaurants and antique shops, to explore the wonderful Cotswolds, this is the ideal centre from which to do this.

Situated just 50 yards from Burford's High Street is the **Royal Oak**, a delightful 17th century inn run by Gary and Sue Duffy. The property has a fascinating history stretching back to around 1615 when one Richard Meryweather owned the then new building that incorporates the present inn. Part of the structure was then an alehouse, and it has been serving ale on and off ever since.

The beamed bar is a pleasant place to enjoy the traditional hand-pulled Wadworth ales and admire the collection of over 400 mugs. The inn also serves good wholesome home-made food at reasonable prices and to the rear there is a patio garden to enjoy in the summer months.

The Royal Oak, Witney Street, Burford Tel: 01933 823278

For those wishing to stay, there are two comfortable en-suite guest rooms which are centrally-heated and equipped with every convenience. The Royal Oak stands on Burford's one-way system and has its own car park, an important asset in this busy town.

Near to the Golf Course, you will find the **Burford Lodge Hotel**, ideally situated for tourists and businessmen alike. The hotel exudes character and charm; it is built of local Cotswold stone and dates back to the early 19th century. All of the rooms are en-suite and equipped to very high standards, with colour television, tea and coffee making facilities and direct-dial telephones. Satellite TV is available in the bar area.

The hotel has a very good restaurant serving an excellent selection of dishes, all of which are home cooked and prepared using the very best local produce whenever possible. The Burford Lodge has a warm and friendly atmosphere which is enhanced by its intimate bar and log fires. This is one of the very best establishments of its type in the area and would make an ideal base for a family holiday, a short romantic break or a business stopover.

There are many places of interest to visit locally, pleasant walks along the river valley to neighbouring villages, fishing on the River Windrush and opportunities for horse riding; keen golfers are well served by the adjacent golf course. This is a fine hotel, one to which you will undoubtedly want to return again and again. You will find it almost equidistant between Oxford (18 miles) and Cheltenham (21 miles) on the A40.

The Burford Lodge Hotel
Oxford Road,
Burford
Tel: 01993 823381

Just outside Burford is **The Cotswold Wild Life Park**. In its 120 acres of park and gardens rhinos, zebras, ostriches, tigers and leopards can all be seen in spacious enclosures. There are walled gardens with tropical birds and monkeys, a reptile house, an aquarium and a butterfly house. There are also picnic areas, an adventure playground and a narrow-gauge railway making it an ideal experience for children of all ages.

ASTHALL

No more than a hamlet, quite near Burford, Asthall is of ancient origins and although it may be only small, it has a marvellous 12th century Church with a unique medieval stone altar. The tower clock on the outside, was made locally and dates back to 1665.

The Jacobean **Manor House** which was built in 1620 has a most interesting recent history. In 1919, David Freeman-Mitford, Lord Redesdale, moved into the Manor together with his wife, son and six daughters who were later to become famous as the Mitford sisters, Nancy, Pamela, Diana, Unity, Jessica and Deborah. In some of her splendid books Nancy Mitford wrote about her family. Deborah Mitford is now the Duchess of Devonshire and Unity became notorious for her attachment to Hitler and Oswald Mosley.

A little tricky to find, Asthall is approached down a narrow country lane off the old A40 between Witney and Burford, just near the Witney by-pass roundabout.

SWINBROOK

Asthall is just south of the little village of Swinbrook, a collection of 17th and 18th century farmhouses and some Victorian cottages built in Tudor style. A great mansion stood in the village, built about 1490 by the Fettiplace family, until 1805, when the last of the family died. No trace of it now remains but the little Church has a fascinating triple-decked monument to three of them, stiff 16th century knights in armour with uncomfortable looking collars, all propped up on one elbow and seemingly about to draw their swords in this unlikely pose. A sight worth the detour before continuing on to Minster Lovell.

MINSTER LOVELL

Minster Lovell Hall was built about 1431-42 and was, in its day, one of the great aristocratic houses of Oxfordshire, the home of the Lovell family. It was arranged around three sides of a courtyard, which was enclosed on the river side by a wall. However, one of the family was a prominent Yorkist during the Wars of the Roses and, after the defeat of Richard III at Bosworth Field, he lost his lands to the Crown.

The house was purchased by the Coke family in 1602, but around the middle of the 18th century the house was dismantled by Thomas Coke, Earl of Leicester, and the ruins became lowly farm buildings. They were rescued from complete disintegration by the Ministry of Works in the 1930s and are now in the care of English Heritage. What is left of the house is extremely picturesque, and it is hard to imagine a better setting than here, beside the river Windrush.

Having seen the comparatively high-tech heating system of the North Leigh Roman Villa, it comes as something of a shock to realise that the Great Hall of this aristocratic house was heated by a fire on a stone hearth in the centre with ventilation provided by openings in the gables of the end walls. One fascinating feature which has survived is the medieval dovecot, complete with nesting boxes, which provided pigeons for the table in a way reminiscent of modern battery henhouses.

CHARTERVILLE

Making our way southwards we pass reminders of an idealistic social experiment at Charterville. All that is left to see are some small cottages with central gables and a towered school, remains of the Chartist Feargus O'Connor's attempt to establish families from the industrialised cities in smallholdings. This early experiment in self-sufficiency began in 1847 but it failed and the estate was sold in 1850.

FILKINS

We continue southwards through **Brize Norton**, home of the great RAF base, and on to Filkins, just off the A361. This tiny Cotswold village is now the home of a flourishing community of craft workers and artists, many of them working in restored 18th century barns. Having been very much aware of the history of the wool industry in the area, it is particularly interesting to visit **Cotswold Woollen Weavers**, where the production process can be followed from fleece to finished cloth.

Located directly opposite St Peter's Church in picturesque Filkins, just north of Lechlade, **Cottage-by-the-Church** is a family home that has been welcoming guests for the past 350 years. This c1650 Grade II listed building was around during the reign of Charles I and was once three cottages and a farmhouse. Though tastefully converted into the modern dwelling that you see before you today, Cottage-by-the-Church still has many of its original features. This rural retreat gleans much of its traditional atmosphere from the heavily beamed ceilings, twisting staircases and inglenook fireplaces that add a distinct air of charm and history to this mellow sandstone building.

Cottage-by-the-Church, Filkins, Lechlade Tel/Fax: 01367 860613

The guests' accommodation comprises two double en-suite bedrooms with patchwork quilts, tasteful furnishings and a complementary tea/ coffee tray. Owned and very capably run by Jane, Cottage-by-the-Church provides a delicious full English breakfast every morning, whilst your evening meals can be enjoyed at either The Lamb Inn or The Five Alls Carvery Restaurant, which are both only five minutes' walk away. Surrounded by a stone-walled cottage garden, filled year round with shrubs and seasonal flowers, there is ample parking at the front of the house where you will find a small courtyard garden complete with its own freshwater well.

KELMSCOTT

From here we head on through **Little Faringdon** for Kelmscott or Kelmscot - opinions differ as to the spelling.

Nowadays William Morris is perhaps best known for his association with the Pre-Raphaelite artists and as a decorator, whose designs for wallpaper and curtain material are still available and popular. He was equally accomplished as a poet and writer, and as a printer. The books he designed and printed are now collectors' items, but his poetry and novels are less suited to modern tastes.

Still less well-known now are Morris' political opinions, formed from his horror of the poverty and ugliness of life for most people in Victorian England. In reaction he turned to the medieval chivalry, Norse heroes and gentler rural patterns of life in times past, and to the future, where he saw socialism as a cure for a world gone awry.

Manor House at Kelmscott was William Morris' country home from 1871 to 1896. It is built of a subtle grey stone, a gabled house near the Thames, dating from about 1570. Morris loved it dearly, and it is the scene of the end of his utopian novel *News from Nowhere*, in which he writes of a world where work has become a sought-after pleasure.

The house, which is open to visitors during the summer, has examples of Morris's work and memorabilia of Dante Gabriel Rosetti, who also stayed there. Rosetti is reputed to have found the village boring, so presumably the fact that he was in love with Morris' wife, Jane, drew him there. Morris himself is buried in the Churchyard, under a tombstone designed by his associate Philip Webb.

The Church itself is interesting, the oldest parts dating from the late 12th century, and the village includes some fine farmhouses from around the end of the 17th and beginning of the 18th centuries.

Another attraction of a trip to Kelmscott is the chance to walk on the towpath beside the Thames using the excellent Thames Walk booklet written by David Sharp and published by the Ramblers' Association. The full walk would take you from Putney to the source of the Thames near Cricklade, but on this occasion just take the opportunity of walking down river to see **Radcot Bridge**. There has been a bridge at or near this site since Saxon times, but the present one is medieval, added to over the centuries. The stone comes from the quarries at Taynton. Upriver you can walk into the lovely Cotswold town of **Lechlade**.

BAMPTON

One of the nicest villages from which you can easily reach all the joys of the Cotswolds, is Bampton, perhaps best known for its Morris Dancers. It is full of history, close to the River Thames, some 12 miles west of Oxford and five miles south of Witney.

Edward the Confessor gave the estate at Bampton to his great friend and tutor, Leofric. It was a busy place then and he was one of the Royal Masons who were required to provide for the King and his household when they visited, but it was an expensive privilege.

The **Church**, along with those of Burford and Witney is among the largest in West Oxfordshire. The oldest parts of the building are probably Saxon. The Church we see now is mostly the result of remodelling carried out about 1270. At this time the spire was added and the aisle built. However, a great deal of Norman work remains and it is interesting to spend some time 'spotting the styles'.

Other buildings well worth a look at are the **Public Library**, formerly the Grammar School, which was completed in 1653. There are a number of houses to be admired, including the stuccoed last Georgian **Manor House** and the **Deanery**, to the west of the Church, which is mostly 17th century. The remains of **Bampton Castle** are incorporated into **Ham Court**. **Weald House** was originally built in the 17th century, but was extensively remodelled about 1730. There are many less grand houses in the centre, around which it is a delight to wander.

WITNEY

Wool was the economic base of life here, just as in so many of the places we have visited in this chapter, and the town is famous for its blankets which have been made here for centuries. The **Blanket Hall** in High Street has on it the arms of the Witney Company of Weavers. It was built for the weighing and measuring of blankets, in an age before rigid standardisation.

There is also a **Butter Cross** in Market Place, a steep roof on rustic-looking stone columns. It was probably built about 1600. Church Green has wide grass verges with pleasant houses set back from the road, and the Church at the south end, **St Mary's**, provides a dramatic focus. Built in the 13th century it is very spacious and the central tower and spire have been compared with Oxford Cathedral in their impact. Some elaborate chantry chapels were added in the 14th century with a clerestory and a parapet with gargoyles around the whole Church in the 15th. Unfortunately the interior, having undergone restoration in the 19th century, is rather a disappointment after the magnificent exterior.

STANDLAKE

Leaving Witney, we turn south on the A415 towards Standlake. Here the **Church** is well worth a visit. It has an unusual west tower, octagonal, with a small spire. The romantically-named **Gaunt House**, half a mile east of the village, was fortified and besieged during the Civil War. Most of what we see now, however, was built in about 1660.

Pause to look at the **New Bridge**, built at the point where the Thames meets the Windrush. Its six pointed arches make a fitting farewell to the current chapter, dominated by the Evenlode and the Windrush.

Tourist Information Centres

Centres in Bold are open all the year round.

Broadway: 1 Cotswold Court 01386 852937
Burford: The Brewery, Sheep Street 01993 823558/823590
Cheltenham: 77 Promenade 01242 522878
Chepstow: The Gatehouse, High Street 01291 623772
Chippenham: The Citadel, Bath Road 01249 657733
Chipping Campden: Woolstaplers' Hall Museum, High Street
     01386 840101
Chipping Norton: The Guildhall 01608 644379/644045
Cirencester: Corn Hall, Market Place 01285 654180
Coleford: 27 Market Place 01594 836307
Gloucester: St Michael's Tower, The Cross 01452 421188
Malmesbury: Town Hall, Market Lane 01666 823748
Newent: The Library, High Street 01531 822145
Northleach: Cotswold Countryside Collection 01451 860715
Stow-on-the-Wold: Hollis House, The Square 01451 831082
Stroud: Subscription Rooms, George Street 01453 765768
Swindon: 37 Regent Street 01793 530328/493007
Tetbury: The Old Court House, 63 Long Street 01666 503552
Tewkesbury: 64 Barton Street 01684 295027
Westbury-upon-Severn: The Library, Edward Street 01373 827158
Winchcombe: Town Hall, High Street 01242 602925
Witney: Town Hall, Market Square 01993 775802
Woodstock: Hensington Road 01993 811038

INDEX

The Hidden Places Series

ORDER FORM

To order more copies of this title or any of the others in this series please complete the order form below and send to:

Travel Publishing Ltd.
7a Apollo House, Calleva Park, Aldermaston, Berks RG7 8TN

Title	Price	Quantity	Value
Channel Islands	£6.99	....	....
Devon & Cornwall	£4.95	....	....
Dorset, Hants & Isle of Wight	£4.95	....	....
East Anglia	£4.95	....	....
Gloucestershire	£6.99	....	....
Heart of England	£4.95	....	....
Lancashire & Cheshire	£4.95	....	....
North Wales	£4.95	....	....
Northumberland & Durham	£4.95	....	....
Somerset, Avon, Glocs & Wilts	£4.95	....	....
South East	£4.95	....	....
South Wales	£4.95	....	....
Thames & Chilterns	£5.99	....	....
Welsh Borders	£5.99	....	....
Yorkshire & Humberside	£4.95	....	....
England	£8.99	....	....
Ireland	£8.99	....	....
Scotland	£8.99	....	....
Wales	£8.99	....	....
TOTAL		_____	_____

For orders of less than 10 copies please add £1 per book for postage & packing. Orders over 10 copies P & P free.

I enclose a cheque for £ .... made payable to Travel Publishing Ltd

NAME   ....

ADDRESS   ....

            ....

POSTCODE   ....